Visual Concept Reviews

Richard O. Straub
University of Michigan, Dearborn

WORTH PUBLISHERS

Acquisitions Editor: Kevin Feyen
Developmental Editors: Betty Probert, Christine Brune
Media Editor: Andrea Musick
Senior Marketing Manager: Kate Nurre
Cover Designer: Lee Mahler
Text Designers: Lee Mahler, Betty Probert
Associate Managing Editor: Tracey Kuehn
Production Manager: Sarah Segal
Composition: TSI Graphics
Printing and Binding: RR Donnelley

ISBN-13: 978-0-7167-2806-1
ISBN-10: 0-7167-2806-0

Worth Publishers
41 Madison Avenue
New York, NY 10010
www.worthpublishers.com

Contents

Preface

These Visual Concept Reviews are designed for use with *Psychology,* Eighth Edition, by David G. Myers. They are intended to supplement the Study Guide in helping you to learn material in the textbook and then to evaluate your understanding of that material. Each chapter includes several review charts, which are in the form of fill-in-the-blank flow charts. Designed to promote a deeper understanding of the conceptual relationships among chapter issues, these review charts cover the major concepts, theories, and psychological issues presented in the corresponding chapter of the textbook. Most charts tell a story, so that you are learning the concepts as applied to real-life situations. Correct answers may be found at the back of the book.

These review charts follow the lead of the text in emphasizing the importance of viewing all human behavior as a product of biological, psychological, and social-cultural influences. Several charts examine a topic, such as drug use, from these different levels of analysis. Sometimes the multiple levels of analysis are included in one chart; sometimes they appear in several charts. Completing all the charts for each chapter will help you to develop a biopsychosocial understanding of these topics.

I would like to thank all the students and instructors who commented on the usefulness of a similar feature in the Study Guide and provided such insightful and useful suggestions for expanding this material into the booklet that you now hold. Thanks, too, to Christine Brune, who reviewed (and improved) each and every chart, to Lee Mahler for the book's beautiful design, and to Tracey Kuehn, Andrea Musick, and Sarah Segal for their dedication and energy in skillfully coordinating various aspects of production. Finally, as is true of every project that I've worked on as a member of the wonderful "Myers team," my heartfelt thanks are due to my editor, Betty Shapiro Probert. Betty helped me develop this idea from its inception and was integral to the content and design development of every chart.

Richard O. Straub

PROLOGUE

REVIEW P.1 : Prescientific Psychology

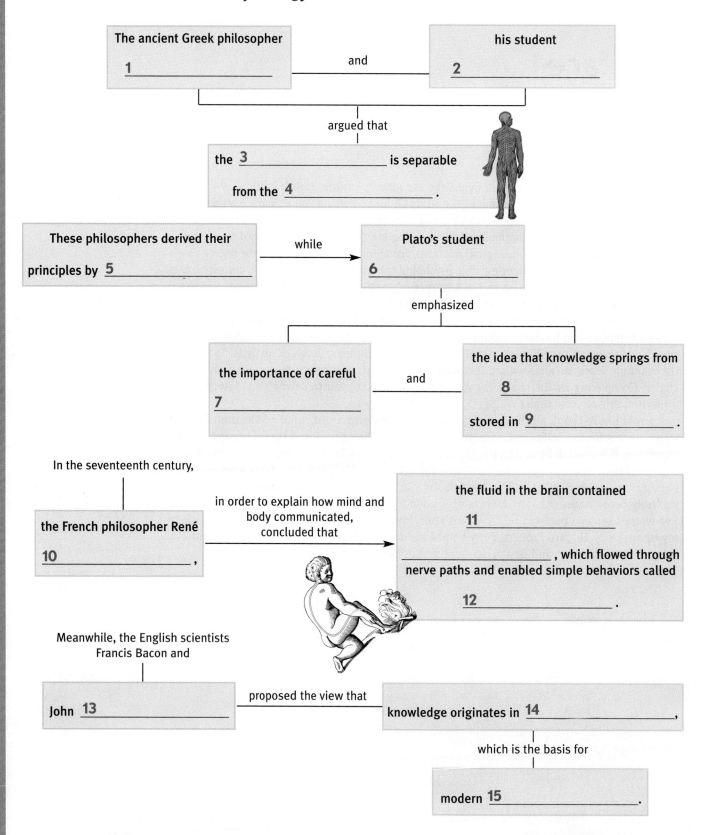

The ancient Greek philosopher

1 _____

and

his student

2 _____

argued that

the **3** _____ is separable

from the **4** _____ .

These philosophers derived their

principles by **5** _____

while

Plato's student

6 _____

emphasized

the importance of careful

7 _____

and

the idea that knowledge springs from

8 _____

stored in **9** _____ .

In the seventeenth century,

the French philosopher René

10 _____ ,

in order to explain how mind and
body communicated,
concluded that

the fluid in the brain contained

11 _____

_____ , which flowed through
nerve paths and enabled simple behaviors called

12 _____ .

Meanwhile, the English scientists
Francis Bacon and

John **13** _____

proposed the view that

knowledge originates in **14** _____ ,

which is the basis for

modern **15** _____ .

Answers may be found in the Appendix at the end of this booklet.

Psychology as we know it began in a laboratory in Germany

in the year 1_____, when Wilhelm

2_____ tried to measure simple

3_____ processes.

His student Edward 4_____ established the school

of psychology called 5_____,
which aimed to discover the elements of the mind. He

used the method known as 6_____,
which involved asking people to look inward.

This method proved to be 7_____
(reliable/unreliable).

At the same time,

another American, William

8_____, focused on how

9_____ and

10_____ processes enable the
human species to survive, establishing the school

of psychology called 11_____.

Beginning in the 1920s,

while Wundt, Titchener, and James engaged in the study of

12_____ life—our inner sensations, images, and feelings—

American psychologists led by

John 13_____

and then by

B. F. 14_____

redefined psychology as

the scientific study of 15_____ _____.

In the 1960s, a softer response to this "mechanistic" view,

16_____ psychology, was pioneered
by Carl Rogers and Abraham Maslow.

Today, with reinvigorated interest in
inner thoughts and feelings,

psychology is defined as the scientific study of

17_____ and

18_____ _____.

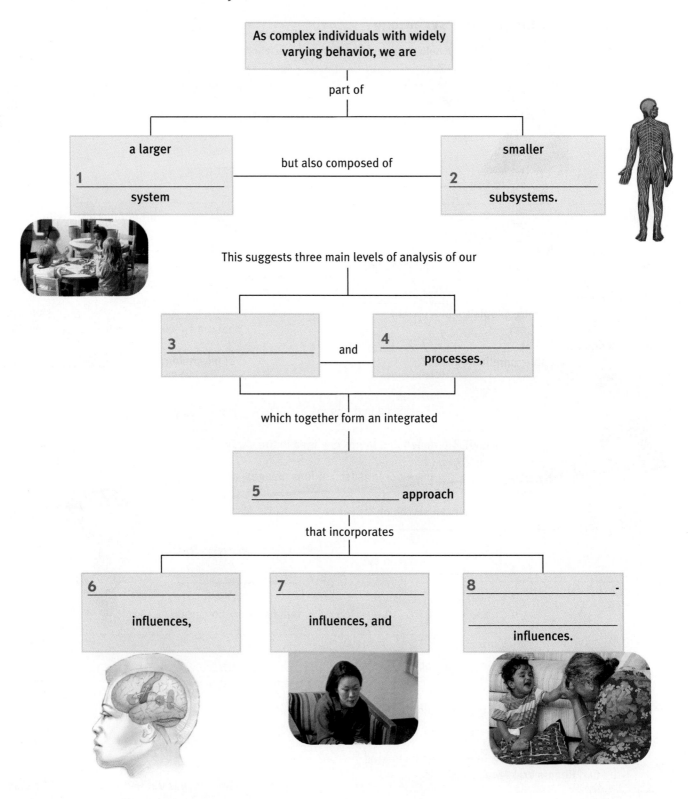

As complex individuals with widely varying behavior, we are

part of

a larger

1 _____

system

but also composed of

smaller

2 _____

subsystems.

This suggests three main levels of analysis of our

3 _____   and   4 _____

processes,

which together form an integrated

5 _____ approach

that incorporates

6 _____

influences,

7 _____

influences, and

8 _____-

_____

influences.

(Continued on next page.)

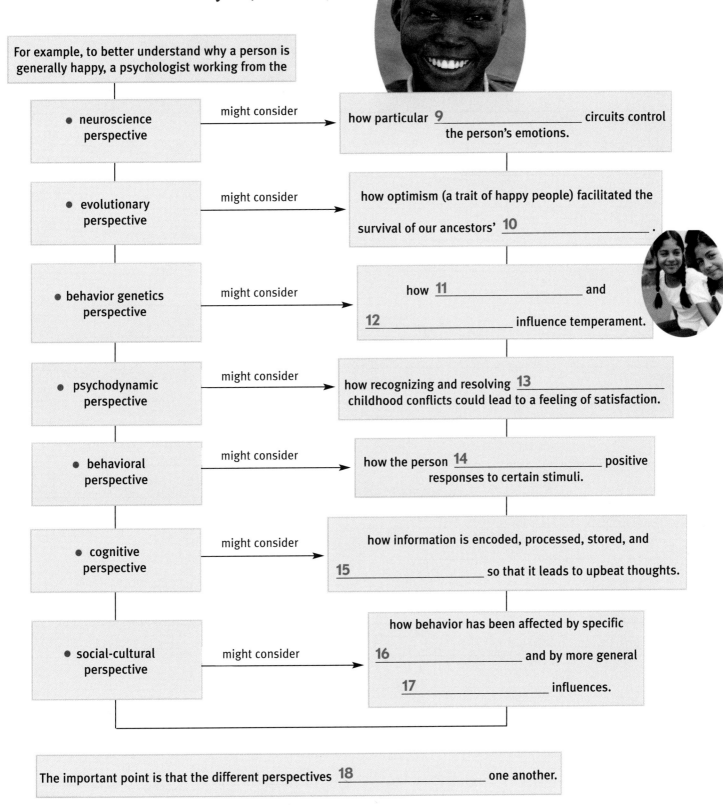

For example, to better understand why a person is generally happy, a psychologist working from the

- **neuroscience perspective** —— might consider —→ how particular 9 _____ circuits control the person's emotions.

- **evolutionary perspective** —— might consider —→ how optimism (a trait of happy people) facilitated the survival of our ancestors' 10 _____ .

- **behavior genetics perspective** —— might consider —→ how 11 _____ and 12 _____ influence temperament.

- **psychodynamic perspective** —— might consider —→ how recognizing and resolving 13 _____ childhood conflicts could lead to a feeling of satisfaction.

- **behavioral perspective** —— might consider —→ how the person 14 _____ positive responses to certain stimuli.

- **cognitive perspective** —— might consider —→ how information is encoded, processed, stored, and 15 _____ so that it leads to upbeat thoughts.

- **social-cultural perspective** —— might consider —→ how behavior has been affected by specific 16 _____ and by more general 17 _____ influences.

The important point is that the different perspectives 18 _____ one another.

Answers may be found in the Appendix at the end of this booklet.

NOTES

NOTES

CHAPTER 1

REVIEW **1.1** : **Science Versus Intuition**

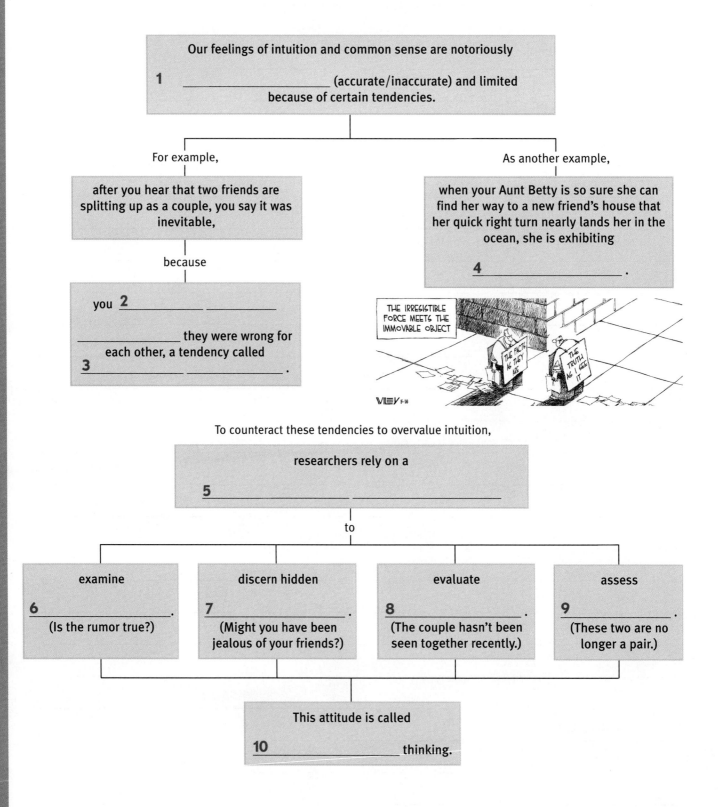

1. Our feelings of intuition and common sense are notoriously _____ (accurate/inaccurate) and limited because of certain tendencies.

For example,

after you hear that two friends are splitting up as a couple, you say it was inevitable,

because

you **2** _____ _____

_____ they were wrong for each other, a tendency called **3** _____ _____.

As another example,

when your Aunt Betty is so sure she can find her way to a new friend's house that her quick right turn nearly lands her in the ocean, she is exhibiting

4 _____ .

THE IRRESISTIBLE FORCE MEETS THE IMMOVABLE OBJECT

THE FACTS AS THEY ARE

THE TRUTH AS I SEE IT

WILEY 5-16

To counteract these tendencies to overvalue intuition,

researchers rely on a

5 _____ _____

to

examine
6 _____ .
(Is the rumor true?)

discern hidden
7 _____ .
(Might you have been jealous of your friends?)

evaluate
8 _____ .
(The couple hasn't been seen together recently.)

assess
9 _____ .
(These two are no longer a pair.)

This attitude is called
10 _____ thinking.

Answers may be found in the Appendix at the end of this booklet.

Dr. Windham contends that contact between people of different ethnicities and cultures increases liking. Using the scientific method,

he develops a scientific **1**_____ that enables him to **2**_____ relevant observations, such as different groups having lunch together, and interpret the meaning of those observations.

The set of principles Dr. Windham has developed

generates testable **3**_____ called **4**_____—for example, that people with such contact score lower on an ingroup bias scale.

Dr. Windham then

conducts **5**_____—for example, administering tests to measure degree of bias before and after contact.

From the results, he accepts,

6_____ , ____or____ **7**_____

his hypothesis.

Dr. Windham reports his findings with precise **8**_____ _____ of concepts that allow others to **9**_____ his research.

PEANUTS

BONK

LUCY, YOU'RE THE WORST PLAYER IN THE HISTORY OF THE GAME!

YOU CAN'T PROVE THAT! YOU SHOULD NEVER SAY THINGS THAT YOU CAN'T PROVE!

IN ALL PROBABILITY, YOU ARE THE WORST PLAYER IN THE HISTORY OF THE GAME!

I CAN ACCEPT THAT..

PEANUTS reprinted by permission of UFS, Inc.

6-17

Dr. Alvarez wants to study increased suicide rates among teenagers. She develops a hypothesis that anxiety leads to depression, which may lead to suicidal behavior. She has a variety of research methods to choose from.

She can focus on one or two extreme situations to educate herself about depression among young people, a method called the

1 _____ _____ ,

which can

suggest 2 _____ for

further study,

but

the information generated may not be

3 _____ of all young people.

Dr. Alvarez could also

conduct a 4 _____ ,

interviewing 5 _____ (a few/ many)

teenagers in 6 _____ (more/less) depth,

creating questions carefully to avoid

7 _____ .

If Dr. Alvarez were to interview only depressed teens and then assume that most teens are depressed, she would be experiencing a phenomenon called the

8 _____ _____

effect.

Instead, Dr. Alvarez will

study a 9 _____

_____ of the teen population, ensuring

that they are 10 _____ of all teens.

Yet another alternative would be for Dr. Alvarez to

study teenagers at school or at play, a method called

11 _____ .

However,

none of the three 12 _____ methods

included on this page, actually

13 _____ why a behavior happens.

(Continued on next page.)

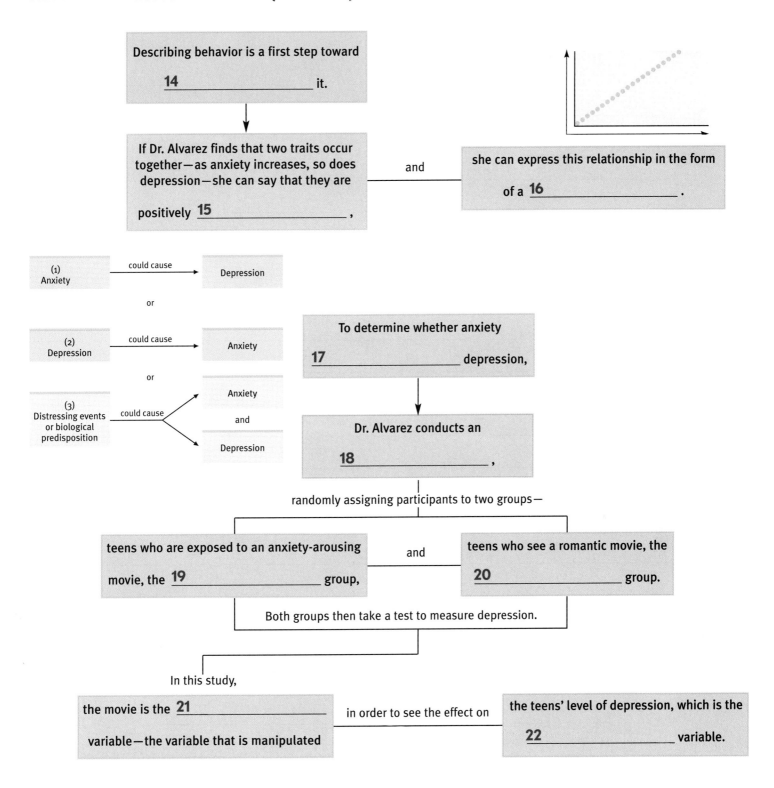

Describing behavior is a first step toward

14 _____ it.

If Dr. Alvarez finds that two traits occur together—as anxiety increases, so does depression—she can say that they are

positively 15 _____ ,

and

she can express this relationship in the form

of a 16 _____ .

(1) Anxiety → could cause → Depression

or

(2) Depression → could cause → Anxiety

or

(3) Distressing events or biological predisposition → could cause → Anxiety and Depression

To determine whether anxiety

17 _____ depression,

Dr. Alvarez conducts an

18 _____ ,

randomly assigning participants to two groups—

teens who are exposed to an anxiety-arousing movie, the 19 _____ group,

and

teens who see a romantic movie, the 20 _____ group.

Both groups then take a test to measure depression.

In this study,

the movie is the 21 _____ variable—the variable that is manipulated

in order to see the effect on

the teens' level of depression, which is the 22 _____ variable.

Answers may be found in the Appendix at the end of this booklet.

NOTES

NOTES

CHAPTER 2

REVIEW 2.1 : **Neural Communication**

As Shay drives down the street, approaching a major intersection, the traffic signal changes to red. For her to perceive the change, light is transmitted to

the backs of her eyes, where 1 _____ neurons can be activated. This information is received on branching fibers called 2 _____ .

When the signal reaches the cell body,

if the 3 _____ signals minus

the 4 _____ signals

exceed

the neuron's 5 _____ , gates

on the neuron's 6 _____ open

and

allow 7 _____ charged

atoms to enter and 8 _____ that part of the membrane.

The resulting 9 _____ _____ travels down the axon,

which is

often coated with an insulating sheath of 10 _____ that increases the speed of transmission.

When the signal reaches the end of the axon,

chemicals called 11 _____ are released into the 12 _____ gap

between

the 13 _____ and the 14 _____ neurons.

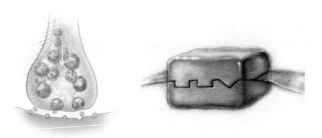

Answers may be found in the Appendix at the end of this booklet.

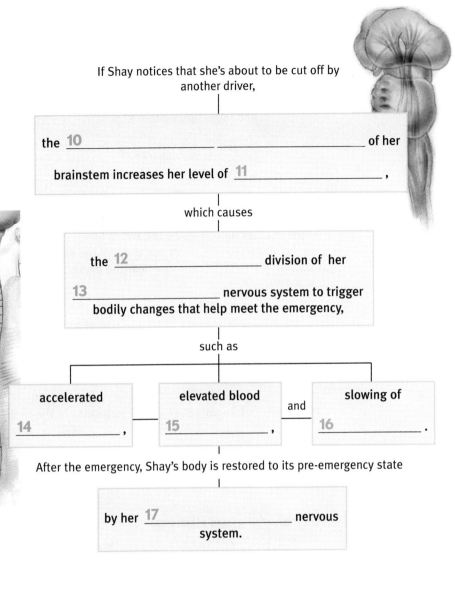

The neural message about the traffic signal travels from Shay's eyes

via

the **1** _____ divison of her

2 _____ nervous system

and is routed by

the brain's sensory switchboard, the

3 _____ ,

to the

4 _____ lobes of her

5 _____

_____ .

When the information about the traffic light reaches Shay's brain, it is

processed by **6** _____ in uncommitted areas of tissue, called

7 _____ areas,

which belong to

the **8** _____

nervous system.

For Shay to stop the car,

her brain must send instructions to her right

leg muscles via **9** _____

neurons that cause her foot to press on the brake.

If Shay notices that she's about to be cut off by another driver,

the **10** _____ _____ of her

brainstem increases her level of **11** _____ ,

which causes

the **12** _____ division of her

13 _____ nervous system to trigger bodily changes that help meet the emergency,

such as

accelerated	elevated blood		slowing of
14 _____ ,	**15** _____ ,	and	**16** _____ .

After the emergency, Shay's body is restored to its pre-emergency state

by her **17** _____ nervous system.

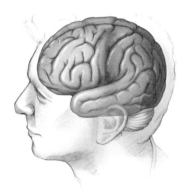

REVIEW 2.3: The Brain

Dave Matthews, the guitarist, is able to play the guitar through the activity of many parts of his brain.

Information is routed from Matthews' eyes, ears, and fingertips via the 1 _____

to the upper-level brain structures:

2 _____
cortex, which enables him to move his fingers,

3 _____
cortex, which enables him to see and feel the strings and hear the music, and

4 _____
areas, which are involved in reading music and playing the guitar.

Information received on one side of the brain crosses to the other side via the 5 _____

_____ , which results in the integrated activity of both sides of the brain.

At the same time, Matthews' body maintains its basic functions.

Heartbeat, breathing, and other vital systems are controlled by the

6 _____ ,

and,

in order to maintain his attention on the guitar, arousal is controlled by the

7 _____ _____ .

Behind Matthews' talent and skills are two more important brain structures:

the 8 _____ , which is involved in his memory of how to play the guitar and of musical scales and time signatures,

and

the 9 _____ , which helps coordinate movements involved in playing the guitar.

Answers may be found in the Appendix at the end of this booklet.

NOTES

NOTES

CHAPTER 3

Jennifer and Brad have decided to have a child. At conception,

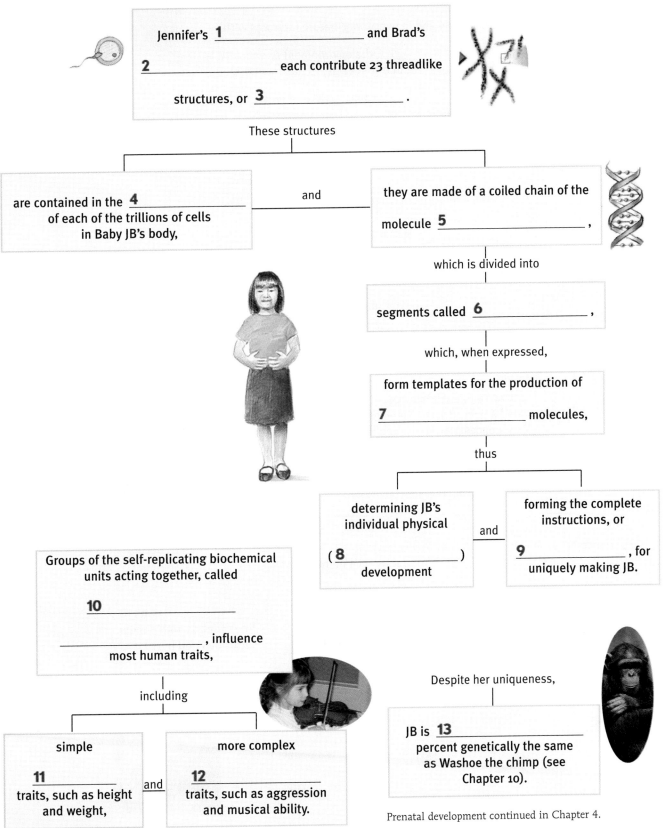

Jennifer's **1**_____ and Brad's

2_____ each contribute 23 threadlike

structures, or **3**_____ .

These structures

are contained in the **4**_____
of each of the trillions of cells
in Baby JB's body,

and

they are made of a coiled chain of the

molecule **5**_____ ,

which is divided into

segments called **6**_____ ,

which, when expressed,

form templates for the production of

7_____ molecules,

thus

determining JB's
individual physical

(**8**_____)

development

and

forming the complete
instructions, or

9_____ , for
uniquely making JB.

Groups of the self-replicating biochemical
units acting together, called

10_____

_____ , influence
most human traits,

including

simple

11_____
traits, such as height
and weight,

and

more complex

12_____
traits, such as aggression
and musical ability.

Despite her uniqueness,

JB is **13**_____
percent genetically the same
as Washoe the chimp (see
Chapter 10).

Prenatal development continued in Chapter 4.

Answers may be found in the Appendix at the end of this booklet.

Nature, Nurture, and Human Diversity

REVIEW 3.2 : **Nature and Nurture**

JB's genetic inheritance, her nature, does not work in a vacuum.

At every level and in every way, nature interacts with

1 _____ , the environment to which JB is exposed. Like the rest of our species, JB has an enormous

2 _____ capacity. As she grows up, she may prefer eating Boston baked beans or refried beans, depending on the tastes she learns from her surrounding

3 _____ .

The interaction of heredity and environment

began when JB was **4** _____ , and

she was affected by the **5** _____

environment of Jen's womb,

including

the **6** _____ she received from what Jen ate and any toxic agents Jen was exposed to. If JB had a twin (BJ), the similarity of their environmental influences prenatally would depend on whether the

twins shared the same **7** _____ .

After birth, JB is affected by several environments:

| Experience helps develop her brain's **8** _____ ; | her family environment has a strong influence on her **9** _____ attitudes, **10** _____ beliefs, and personal manners; | peer influence occurs through a **11** _____ _____ , as JB finds friends with similar attitudes and interests; |

and finally,

JB follows the rules of accepted and expected behavior, or

12 _____ , of her culture.

Answers may be found in the Appendix at the end of this booklet.

REVIEW 3.3: Gender Differences

Now suppose that JB has a brother Bruno, who is a few years younger.
Assume that JB and Bruno are an average female and male.

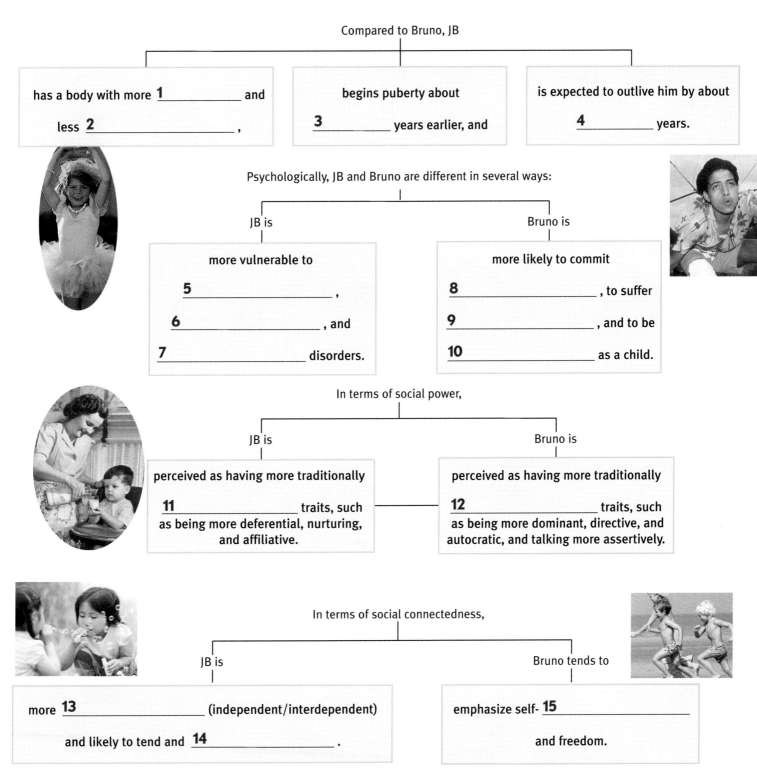

Compared to Bruno, JB

has a body with more **1**_____ and

less **2**_____ ,

begins puberty about

3_____ years earlier, and

is expected to outlive him by about

4_____ years.

Psychologically, JB and Bruno are different in several ways:

JB is

more vulnerable to

5_____ ,

6_____ , and

7_____ disorders.

Bruno is

more likely to commit

8_____ , to suffer

9_____ , and to be

10_____ as a child.

In terms of social power,

JB is

perceived as having more traditionally

11_____ traits, such
as being more deferential, nurturing,
and affiliative.

Bruno is

perceived as having more traditionally

12_____ traits, such
as being more dominant, directive, and
autocratic, and talking more assertively.

In terms of social connectedness,

JB is

more **13**_____ (independent/interdependent)

and likely to tend and **14**_____ .

Bruno tends to

emphasize self- **15**_____

and freedom.

Answers may be found in the Appendix at the end of this booklet.

NOTES

NOTES

CHAPTER 4

REVIEW 4.1 : Physical Development

Jorge and Sonya Nuñez have a son named Felipe.

Felipe started out as a fertilized egg, or 1 _____, whose cells quickly began to 2 _____.

Two weeks into 3 _____ development, his organs began to form and function, and he was referred to as an 4 _____.

As Felipe became more human in appearance, about 9 weeks after conception, he was called a 5 _____.

Throughout this process,

Felipe's genes interacted with the 6 _____, and Felipe was protected by the 7 _____, which prevented many harmful substances from reaching him,

and

because Sonya didn't drink alcohol, Felipe was NOT exposed to this harmful 8 _____

and will not be at risk of developing 9 _____ _____ _____.

As a newborn,

Felipe came equipped with a variety of 10 _____ suited to survival,

including

the tendency to turn toward Sonya when she touched him on the cheek, called the 11 _____ _____.

Felipe is now an infant, and his biological and psychological development continues,

depending to a large extent on the rapid development of his brain's 12 _____ lobes,

with

the last areas of the brain to develop being those linked with thinking, memory, and language—the 13 _____ areas of the cortex.

As his genes continue to direct his biological growth through the process called 14 _____,

Felipe begins to sit, crawl, stand, walk, and then run. This 15 _____ of motor development is universal; the 16 _____ is not.

(Continued on next page.)

Felipe is now a teenager, an adolescent who

has just attained sexual maturity, or 17 _____ . His younger sister, Elena,

has reached the same stage, but she is only 18 _____ years old.

During the growth spurt that follows, their reproductive organs—his testes and her ovaries, or

19 _____ _____

_____ —develop dramatically,

while

Elena's breasts and hips and Felipe's voice and body hair, or 20 _____ _____

_____ , also begin to develop.

When Jorge and Sonya criticize their children's clothing, hairstyle, or the friends they bring home, Felipe storms outside, slamming the door behind him, and Elena retreats to her room, iPod in hand.

Their behavior can be blamed in part on the early development of the brain's emotional

21 _____ _____ .

Fortunately,

this is followed by selective 22 _____ of unused neurons and connections and the growth of fatty

23 _____ tissue in the frontal lobes, which leads to improved judgment and impulse control.

Adulthood brings benefits and challenges:

Both Felipe and Elena can maintain physical vigor if

they have good 24 _____ habits.

For Elena,

biological aging is signaled by the end of menstruation,

or 25 _____ , which is accompanied by

a reduction in the hormone 26 _____ .

For Felipe,

there is no comparable loss of 27 _____ , but there is a gradual decline in sperm count and lower

levels of the hormone 28 _____ .

In old age, their 29 _____ systems weaken, and they are 30 _____ (more/less)

susceptible to life-threatening illnesses and 31 _____ (more/less) susceptible to short-term illnesses.

The Nuñez family lives in the city. Every year, beginning when the children are very young, they vacation on a farm.

In the city, the children see many dogs and develop a concept, or 1_____ , for four-legged animals. On the farm, they see pigs and goats and try to 2_____ these animals into their dog concept,

but

Sonya corrects them and identifies the animals as separate concepts, so the children have to 3_____ their schemas to fit their new experiences.

Also, according to Jean 4_____ , the mind develops through a series of 5_____ as we continually modify our thinking to fit the particulars of new experiences.

At age 1, Elena

puts all objects—rattles, keys, anything within reach—into her mouth. She's in the 6_____ stage.

At age 3, Felipe

has an imaginary friend and can describe events with words, and so is in the 8_____ stage.

If the rattle is hidden, Elena knows it's still there somewhere and will search for it. She has developed

7_____ .

He doesn't understand that water in an inverted beaker could be the same amount as water in a rightside-up beaker—the concept of 9_____ —and when he covers his eyes, he thinks no one can see him, which means he is

10_____ .

When Elena is 6 and Felipe is 8,

they can understand that the two beakers contain the same amount, and so they are in the 11_____ _____ stage.

According to Lawrence 12_____ , Felipe and Elena have probably developed a 13_____ morality based on a desire to avoid punishment or gain rewards.

I better share this toy or Mommy will be mad.

26

(Continued on next page.)

With adolescence comes newfound
reasoning abilities and a strong moral sense:

> Now in the **14** _____
>
> _____ stage, Felipe and Elena
> think about such abstract concepts as war, justice,
> and democracy,

and

> their morality has evolved to a more
>
> **15** _____ level, based on
>
> upholding laws and obeying rules.

Jorge and Sonya, who are now in their 50s, join their children,
who are in their 20s, in a memory test.

> Research indicates that Felipe and Elena will be better
>
> at **16** _____ (recalling/recognizing)
> information, while Jorge and Sonya will excel at
>
> **17** _____ (recalling/recognizing)
> information.

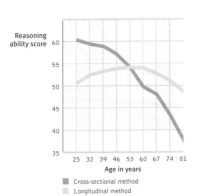
I don't care if it is the law,
it's not right and it's not fair!

Number
of words
remembered

24 ⎯

20 ⎯

Number of words
recognized is stable
with age

16 ⎯

12 ⎯

8 ⎯

Number of words
recalled declines
with age

4 ⎯

0 ⎯

20   30   40   50   60   70

Age in years

Also

> Mom and Pop's ability to solve Sudoku puzzles (to
> reason speedily), reflected in their
>
> **18** _____ intelligence, will decline,

while

> their ability to win at Scrabble (to have a large
> vocabulary), reflected in their
>
> **19** _____ intelligence, will increase.

At first, researchers thought intelligence generally
declined with age. This was because

> they compared the test scores of people of different
>
> ages, using the **20** _____-
>
> _____ method,

while

> newer research, using the **21** _____
>
> method, showed that intelligence remains stable until
> late in life.

Reasoning
ability score

60 ⎯

55 ⎯

50 ⎯

45 ⎯

40 ⎯

35 ⎯

25 32 39 46 53 60 67 74 81

Age in years

▢ Cross-sectional method
▢ Longitudinal method

Answers may be found in the Appendix at the end of this booklet.

Many years later, Elena's daughter Leah asks her 90-year-old grandmother Sonya about her early life. Sonya tells Leah: "I had a wonderful childhood,

with

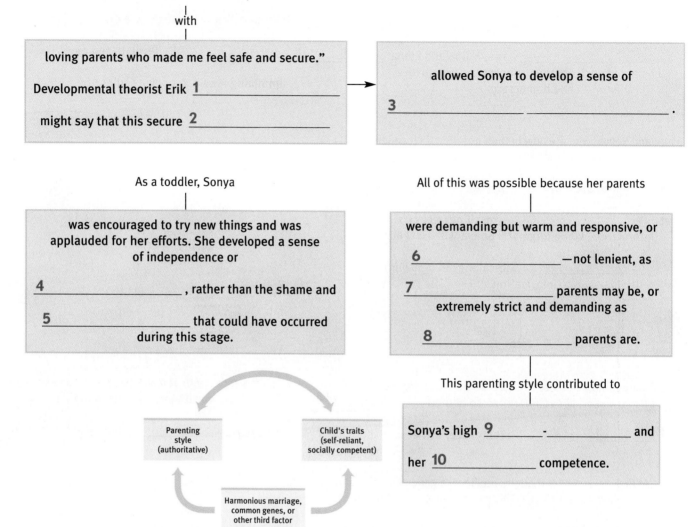

loving parents who made me feel safe and secure."

Developmental theorist Erik **1**_____

might say that this secure **2**_____

allowed Sonya to develop a sense of

3_____ _____ .

As a toddler, Sonya

was encouraged to try new things and was applauded for her efforts. She developed a sense of independence or

4_____ , rather than the shame and

5_____ that could have occurred during this stage.

All of this was possible because her parents

were demanding but warm and responsive, or

6_____—not lenient, as

7_____ parents may be, or extremely strict and demanding as

8_____ parents are.

This parenting style contributed to

Sonya's high **9**_____-_____ and

her **10**_____ competence.

Parenting style (authoritative)

Child's traits (self-reliant, socially competent)

Harmonious marriage, common genes, or other third factor

As a child in school, when Sonya began learning how to read and write,

she developed a sense of **11**_____ rather than inferiority and a clear sense of her own identity and personal worth, or a

12_____-_____ .

(Continued on next page.)

As a teenager,

Sonya was aggressive and opinionated with her friends but shy and agreeable with her parents until she finally merged these different selves into a

consistent 13 _____ .

During high school, Sonya moved from small groups of girlfriends to mixed groups of boys and girls to dating one boy. Along the way,

she learned about relationships and developed a

capacity for 14 _____ , thus avoiding

a sense of social 15 _____ .

Then,

following the culturally preferred timing of social

events, or the 16 _____ _____ , she married her childhood sweetheart, Jorge, after college. They both had fulfilling careers while raising a loving, caring family.

Sonya says, "These contributions to the world and to future generations have

given Jorge and me a strong sense of 17 _____ , unlike mean old Mr. Ramirez across the street, whose life has been purposeless." Erikson would say Ramirez is

18 _____ .

Sonya continued, "As your grandfather and I look back on our lives, we are content.

Our lives have been meaningful and worthwhile; we

have a sense of 19 _____ rather than the despair felt by Mr. Ramirez."

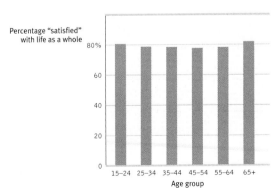

Percentage "satisfied" with life as a whole

Age group

Answers may be found in the Appendix at the end of this booklet.

29

NOTES

NOTES

CHAPTER 5

REVIEW 5.1 : Vision

400	500	600		

Part of spectrum visible to humans

X-rays	Ultra-violet		Infrared rays	Radar

Jamail is a software engineer who is animating a new soccer computer game.

The visible light from the computer screen, which is only a small portion of the 1 _____ spectrum of energy,

has two physical characteristics:

the distance from one wave peak to the next is its 2 _____ ,

which determines

the 3 _____ —for example, the blue shorts and green background Jamail has chosen for his animation—

and

the height, or 4 _____ , from peak to trough of the wave,

which determines

the amount of energy in a light wave, or its 5 _____ , which we perceive as brightness.

For Jamail's eyes to see, they must transform particles of light energy into colorful objects in this sequence:

Light enters Jamail's eyes through the protective 6 _____

and then

passes through a small opening, the 7 _____ ,

which

is regulated by a colored muscle, the 8 _____ .

Next,

light passes through the 9 _____ ,

which,

by a process called 10 _____ ,

focuses

the light on the eye's 11 _____ .

When the image from the computer screen reaches Jamail's retina, it stimulates two receptor cells:

the 12 _____ , in the periphery, for black-and-white vision,

and

the 13 _____ , in the fovea, for color vision,

which

stimulate the 14 _____ cells,

which then

activate the 15 _____ cells,

whose axons form the 16 _____ nerve

that

carries information to Jamail's 17 _____ .

Answers may be found in the Appendix at the end of this booklet.

REVIEW 5.2 : **Hearing**

As Jamail programs the new soccer computer game, he is careful to adjust the sound track in order to regulate the sound waves' two physical characteristics:

the waves' length, which determines their **1** _____ ,

which

we perceive as **2** _____ ,

and

the strength, or **3** _____ , of the waves,

which

we perceive as **4** _____ .

Jamail is able to perceive these psychological properties of sound, because the sound waves enter his outer ear and

are channeled through the **5** _____ _____ to the membrane that vibrates in response to the pressure, which is called the **6** _____ .

The vibrations are then transmitted

to three tiny bones: the **7** _____ , **8** _____ , and **9** _____ ,

which

cause the **10** _____ _____ of the snail-shaped tube called the **11** _____ to vibrate.

In this tube, the vibrations from Jamail's characters' screams, grunts, and groans

cause fluid to move, creating ripples in the **12** _____ _____ ,

which

is lined with **13** _____ _____ that bend,

triggering

impulses in **14** _____ fibers that form the **15** _____ nerve,

which

sends the information to the auditory **16** _____ in the brain's **17** _____ lobe.

REVIEW 5.3: **Pain**

Jamail has spent so many hours on the computer, hand wrapped around the mouse, that his middle fingers feel numb and pain is shooting up his arm.

According to the **1** _____-

_____ theory, Jamail's spinal cord contains two types of fibers:

small fibers, which **2** _____ (open/close) the gate to the brain, so that Jamail **3** _____ (does/does not) feel pain,

and

large fibers, which **4** _____ (open/close) the gate to the brain, so that Jamail **5** _____ (does/does not) feel pain.

Because Jamail has an approaching deadline, he plods on.

He belongs to a **6** _____ that encourages stoicism in the face of pain.

Also,

he is **7** _____ from the pain by thoughts of the deadline as well as by the cool snow scenes in the cyber environment in which he is operating to create his game,

which

is similar to **8** _____- reality pain control.

Answers may be found in the Appendix at the end of this booklet.

It's time for Jamail to take a break. He closes his eyes to relax, but the phone, which is to the left of him, rings. With his eyes still closed, he is able to pick up the phone. He does this

because

the 1 _____ _____ difference of the sound reaching his two ears

tells

his sense of 2 _____ where to move his hand.

Jamail's ability illustrates the concept that one sense may influence another, which is called

3 _____ _____ .

This principle works for all of his senses. For example, Jamail finishes talking to his friend and goes to the kitchen for a snack,

where the smell of freshly baked bread activates the

receptors in the 4 _____ membrane,

which

transmits electric signals to higher regions of the brain by way of converged

5 _____ .

Because the receptors for smell are located

near the brain's ancient 6 _____ centers, the smell of the bread

evokes

7 _____ of his childhood, when his mother spent Saturdays baking for the family.

Jamail takes a piece of bread.

Adding to the smell and texture of the bread,

his taste 8 _____ give him the flavor of banana bread,

and

this information is sent to the brain's

9 _____ lobe, which is near where olfactory information is received.

NOTES

NOTES

CHAPTER 6

REVIEW 6.1 : **Three-Dimensional Perception**

Bethany is a member of Gamma University's bowling team, and she's been selected to play against nearby Alpha University. Besides physical dexterity, she

depends on 1 _____ perception to estimate the distance and angle of the ball from the pins she is trying to knock down.

Visual cues are the source of this perception.

Using both eyes, the 2 _____ cues help Bethany bowl a great game.

The brain compares the difference, or

3 _____ _____ , of the images from her right and left eyes, telling her that the 1 pin is closer than the 5 pin behind it.

The inward turning of the eye, required for focusing, which is called

4 _____ , also tells her that the 1 pin is closer.

Each eye also provides 5 _____ cues that contribute to her accurate bowling.

For example, she knows that the 8 pin is farther away from her than the 5 pin because

of the difference in the 6 _____

_____ of the images that the bowling pins cast on her retina

and

the fact that the 5 pin appears

7 _____ (lighter/darker) than the 8 pin,

while

the 8 pin is 8 _____ (higher/lower) in her field of vision.

Also, the 5 pin partially blocks her view of the

8 pin, a cue called 9 _____ .

Answers may be found in the Appendix at the end of this booklet.

REVIEW 6.2 : **Perceptual Interpretation**

Kurt is now a college junior with perfect vision. However, he was born with

an opaque lens, or ___1_____ , in each eye, which were surgically corrected when he was an infant.

If Kurt's vision had not been restored until he was an adult,

philosopher Immanuel ___2_____ would have predicted that Kurt would have difficulty visually identifying objects learned from touch,

while

philosopher John ___3_____ , who believed that knowledge comes from ___4_____ ways of organizing sensory information, would have disagreed.

Today, Kurt is a criminal science major because his goal is to work in law enforcement. His friends tease him that

he has a mental predisposition, or ___5_____ _____ , to "see" crime and violence everywhere he looks.

A psychologist might say that his education and interests have shaped

his perceptual concepts, or ___6_____ .

For example

when shown the reversible ___7_____- _____ drawing at left, which can be seen as either people charging or arrowheads,

Kurt readily perceives

"violent people charging" as the ___8_____ and the white arrowheads as the ___9_____ .

Answers may be found in the Appendix at the end of this booklet.   39

NOTES

NOTES

CHAPTER 7

REVIEW 7.1 : **Biological Rhythms and Sleep**

This doctor worked the night shift for 6 months and has now switched to days. Clearly, he has not yet succeeded

in resetting his 24-hour **1** _____

_____ . He would be well advised
to spend some time outdoors during the day

because

bright light activates **2** _____

in his eyes' **3** _____ ,

which

trigger signals to the brain's

4 _____ nucleus,

causing

the **5** _____ gland to
decrease production of the sleep-

inducing hormone **6** _____ .

Being sleep deprived, this doctor

may experience a depressed **7** _____

system, impaired **8** _____ ,
and impaired concentration—not what you want in
someone who is treating an illness or injury.

So, the doctor finally gets some sleep,
passing through the five sleep stages,

preceded by

the relaxed, awake state that is characterized with regular

9 _____ waves.

In Stage 1, he may feel
he is falling, a

10 _____
sensation,

and

having false sensory
experiences, or

11 _____ .

In Stage 2, his brain
generates bursts of
rapid activity, or sleep

12 _____ .

In Stages 3 and 4,

13 _____

sleep, he experiences

large, slow

14 _____
waves.

When waves become
rapid and saw-toothed
and eyes dart about, he
has entered

15 _____ sleep,

where

he **16** _____
of making a major
medical breakthrough.

Answers may be found in the Appendix at the end of this booklet.

Review 7.2 : **Drug Abuse**

Jack believes that three main influences may contribute to his
neighbor Brian's heavy drinking:

Brian's parents have a history
of alcoholism, so he may have

a **1**_____
predisposition.

Brian's life has been significantly
disrupted by the drinking, which
suggests an underlying

2_____ .

Brian spends a lot of time with friends
at the local bar, which suggests that

3_____
influence is also significant.

Since Jack moved in 5 years ago, Brian's drinking
has increased, most likely because

a few beers have less effect on Brian (he's

developed a **4**_____
for alcohol),

and

his brain is experiencing

5_____ as it
attempts to counteract the effects of the alcohol.

In addition,

to cope with stress, Brian has at least a
few beers every day, indicating that he has

developed **6**_____
dependence,

while

his daily cravings for alcohol suggest that
he may also have developed a

7_____
dependence.

Jack is particularly worried about the effects on Brian's mind and body:

Alcohol is a kind of psychoactive drug called a **8**_____ ,

because it

physically slows down activity in the **9**_____ nervous system, causes Brian's

brain to **10**_____ (enlarge/shrink), and boosts activity in the brain's

11_____ reward system.

Psychologically, alcohol lowers **12**_____ , impairs judgment and

13_____ , and causes Brian to lose self- **14**_____ .

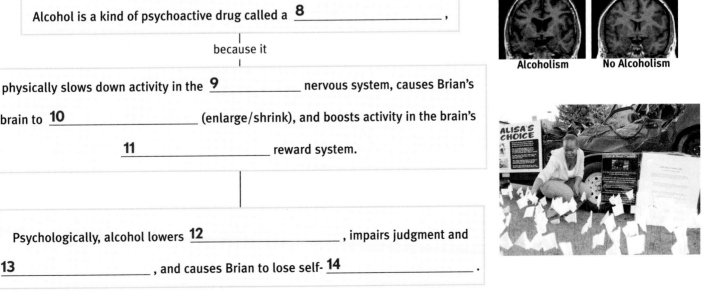

Alcoholism   No Alcoholism

ALISA'S CHOICE

NOTES

NOTES

CHAPTER 8

REVIEW 8.1 : Classical Conditioning

Antonia lives in Alaska. She loves walking through falling snow and feeling the wet snowflakes on her face.

Whenever a snowflake—the 1 _____ _____—falls into her eye,

it triggers

an eyeblink, which is the 2 _____ _____ .

Coincidentally, each time a snowflake falls into her eye, the school bell rings, which is a 3 _____ _____ .

And,

after several pairings with the snowflake in the eye, the bell also begins to trigger an eyeblink, and so it is now the 4 _____ _____ .

This is the 5 _____ stage of classical conditioning.

While in school, the bell rings between class periods, but of course there are no snowflakes, which results in

6 _____ of Antonia's eyeblink response.

At recess, another snowflake falls into her eye just as the warning bell rings to go back inside. When the final bell rings a few minutes later, Antonia finds herself blinking,

which shows that

she has experienced 7 _____ _____ of her eyeblink response to the bell.

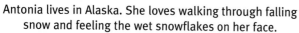

Strong

Acquisition
(CS + US)

Extinction
(CS alone)

Spontaneous
recovery of CR

Strength
of CR

Extinction
(CS alone)

Weak

Pause

Time

If a clock chime similar to the original school bell were to be presented,

responding with the eyeblink would represent

Not responding to the similar stimulus would represent

8 _____

9 _____ .

Answers may be found in the Appendix at the end of this booklet.

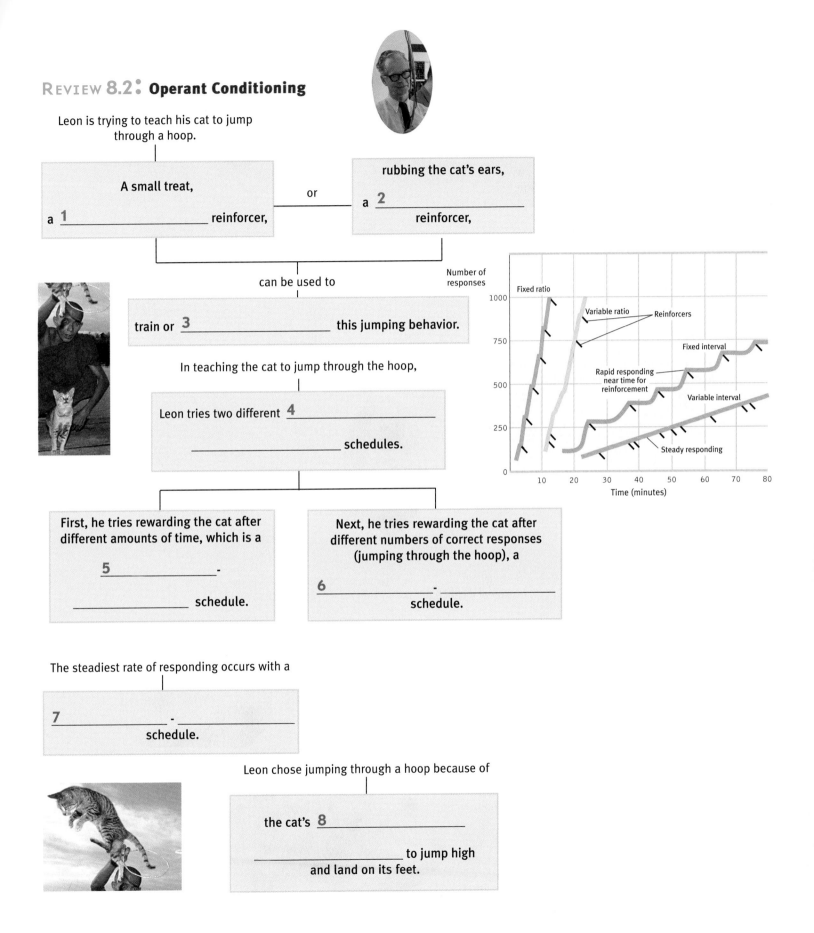

REVIEW 8.2: **Operant Conditioning**

Leon is trying to teach his cat to jump through a hoop.

A small treat,

or

a 1 _____ reinforcer,

rubbing the cat's ears,

a 2 _____

reinforcer,

can be used to

train or 3 _____ this jumping behavior.

In teaching the cat to jump through the hoop,

Leon tries two different 4 _____

_____ schedules.

First, he tries rewarding the cat after different amounts of time, which is a

5 _____-

_____ schedule.

Next, he tries rewarding the cat after different numbers of correct responses (jumping through the hoop), a

6 _____-_____ schedule.

Number of responses

1000

Fixed ratio

Variable ratio — Reinforcers

750

Fixed interval

Rapid responding near time for reinforcement

500

Variable interval

250

Steady responding

0

10 20 30 40 50 60 70 80

Time (minutes)

The steadiest rate of responding occurs with a

7 _____-_____ schedule.

Leon chose jumping through a hoop because of

the cat's 8 _____

_____ to jump high and land on its feet.

Answers may be found in the Appendix at the end of this booklet. 47

REVIEW 8.3: **Learning by Observation**

According to pioneering researcher Albert

1 _____ , we learn not
only by association

but also by

2 _____ the behavior
of people

who are

successful, admirable, and

3 _____ to us.

For example, during holiday breaks Lionel watches *Monday Night Raw,* a World Wrestling Entertainment extravaganza,

which

4 _____ (increases/decreases) his aggressive tendencies.

His brother Michael won't watch the wrestling, because he feels the pain of a choke hold, for example, as reflected in

his brain's 5 _____

_____ .

Empathy

Instead, Michael spends time with Grandma, who cooks for the poor during the holiday season,

helping Michael to learn

6 _____ behavior.

Answers may be found in the Appendix at the end of this booklet.

NOTES

NOTES

REVIEW 9.1 : **Information Processing**

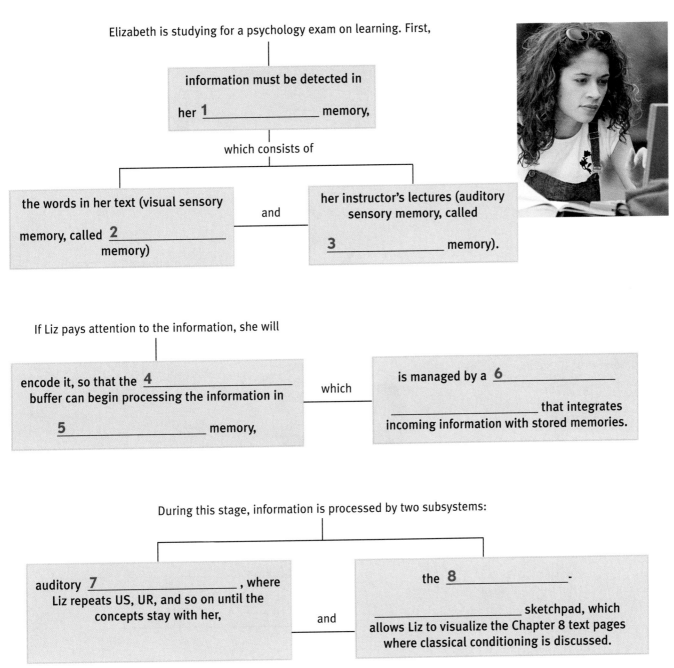

Elizabeth is studying for a psychology exam on learning. First,

information must be detected in

her **1**_____ memory,

which consists of

the words in her text (visual sensory

memory, called **2**_____
memory)

and

her instructor's lectures (auditory
sensory memory, called

3_____ memory).

If Liz pays attention to the information, she will

encode it, so that the **4**_____
buffer can begin processing the information in

5_____ memory,

which

is managed by a **6**_____

_____ that integrates
incoming information with stored memories.

During this stage, information is processed by two subsystems:

auditory **7**_____ , where
Liz repeats US, UR, and so on until the
concepts stay with her,

and

the **8**_____-

_____ sketchpad, which
allows Liz to visualize the Chapter 8 text pages
where classical conditioning is discussed.

(Continued on next page.)

REVIEW **9.1** : **Information Processing** (*continued*)

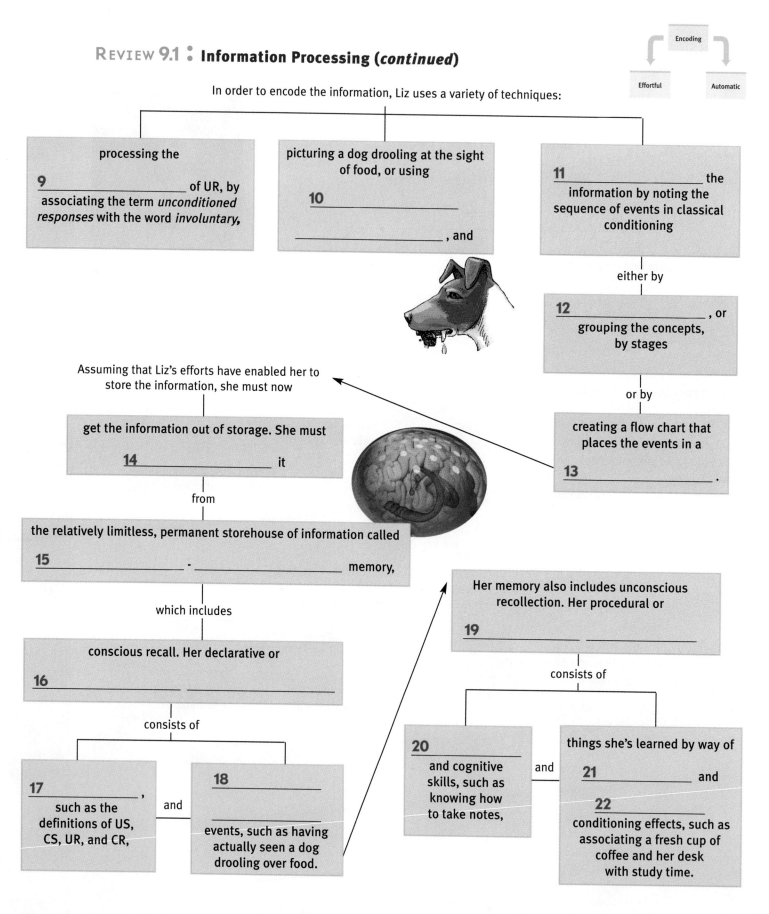

Encoding

Effortful   Automatic

In order to encode the information, Liz uses a variety of techniques:

processing the

9 _____ of UR, by associating the term *unconditioned responses* with the word *involuntary*,

picturing a dog drooling at the sight of food, or using

10 _____

_____ , and

11 _____ the information by noting the sequence of events in classical conditioning

either by

12 _____ , or grouping the concepts, by stages

or by

creating a flow chart that places the events in a

13 _____ .

Assuming that Liz's efforts have enabled her to store the information, she must now

get the information out of storage. She must

14 _____ it

from

the relatively limitless, permanent storehouse of information called

15 _____ - _____ memory,

which includes

conscious recall. Her declarative or

16 _____ _____

consists of

17 _____ , such as the definitions of US, CS, UR, and CR,

and

18 _____

_____ events, such as having actually seen a dog drooling over food.

Her memory also includes unconscious recollection. Her procedural or

19 _____ _____

consists of

20 _____ and cognitive skills, such as knowing how to take notes,

and

things she's learned by way of

21 _____ and

22 _____ conditioning effects, such as associating a fresh cup of coffee and her desk with study time.

Answers may be found in the Appendix at the end of this booklet.

REVIEW **9.2 : Forgetting**

Information bits

As a senior member of her high school swim team, Melissa is rewarded with a large locker. She learns the new combination,

21 left . . .
5 right . . .
43 left

|
but

then she can't remember the code for the old padlock on her bike; this is an example of

1 _____ _____ .

After practice. while Melissa is struggling with the padlock, two new team members pass by. She says,

"Hi, Rebecca," but realizes she's now the victim of

2 _____ _____ ,

because Rebecca is the name of a teammate who graduated last year.

Both of these reasons for forgetting are

forms of **3** _____ failure, because in both cases, the information was in long-term memory.

An alternative explanation for Melissa's memory problems is that

she never actually **4** _____ the new information into long-term memory.

During practice, the coach referred to a pep talk, which she said Melissa had given before last year's championship meet. But,

|

in fact, Rebecca had given the pep talk. Melissa's coach is suffering from

5 _____ amnesia,

possibly because

Melissa had provided

6 _____

information by referring to her ability to urge her teammates on.

Melissa's Aunt Kate is so fearful of water that she can't attend her niece's swim meets,

|
but

she doesn't know why she is fearful.

Sigmund **7** _____
might have suggested

that

Kate has **8** _____
a traumatic childhood incident, which left her with this disruptive fear.

Contemporary researchers **9** _____
(agree/disagree) with the psychoanalytic view of forgetting.

NOTES

NOTES

CHAPTER **10**

REVIEW **10.1** : **Problem Solving**

Pierre is applying to the Delicioso Culinary Institute. To qualify, he must prepare a special recipe of his own design, so he practices at home.

At first, he tries mixing different ingredients to create a unique pasta sauce. This hit-and-miss method is referred to as

1 _____ and 2 _____ .

After tossing out several "yucky" recipes, he learns more about which herbs mix well together and in what order,

and so he writes out a recipe, a step-by-step

procedure, or 3 _____ , for an unbelievably "delicioso" pasta sauce.

Pierre takes the test, is accepted by the Institute, and, several years later, is hired as "Chef to the Stars."

Guided by his experience, Pierre uses a simple

thinking strategy, or 4 _____ , to create many more awesome recipes,

and

occasionally, he creates a recipe that comes to him

in a flash of inspiration, or 5 _____ .

While Pierre is successfully building a career as a world-renowned chef, his friend André (who also wants to be a chef) has not done well.

André's attempts to create original recipes have been hindered by his inability to look at a problem from

a fresh perspective. This 6 _____

may be in the form of

a 7 _____ _____ , or a tendency to approach a problem with what has worked before—for example, always broiling pork chops when pan-frying might work well—

or

8 _____ _____ , a tendency to think of things in terms of their usual functions—for example, thinking basil can be used only for flavoring spaghetti sauce when it's also "delicioso" in meat loaf.

André blames his failure on his own misuse of problem-solving techniques.

In creating recipes, he was affected by the

9 _____ _____ , because he only tried the combinations that came readily to mind rather than thinking outside the box about other possibilities.

He was also overly affected by the 10 _____

_____ when he chose only the ingredients that matched his prototype for pasta sauces.

Answers may be found in the Appendix at the end of this booklet.

REVIEW 10.2 : Language Development

Erika and Jason have twins: Spencer was born with normal hearing, and Sheila was born deaf. Erika and Jason have therefore learned American Sign Language.

The children **1** _____ (did/did not) pass through the same sequence of stages of language development,

which began

at 2 or 3 months of age, with **2** _____ , or uttering sounds that can be found in all languages.

By their second birthday,

both children had entered into the **3** _____ - _____ stage ,

in which

Spencer's words and Sheila's hand signs are mostly **4** _____ and **5** _____ ,

which

is referred to as **6** _____ _____ .

In Spencer's spoken words,

the basic sounds, such as *ba, da,* and *ma,* are called **7** _____ ,

and

those sounds form the smallest unit of meaningful language, such as *dad,* which is a **8** _____ .

Sounds and words derive meaning based on the set of language rules we call **9** _____ . The rules for ordering words are referred to as the **10** _____ of the language's grammar.

"Got idea. Talk better. Combine words. Make sentences."

(Continued on the next page.)

Psychologists agree that Spencer and Sheila's rapid acquisition of productive language

depended on their exposure to language during a 11 _____ _____ of development.

Psychologists disagree on how language develops.

Behaviorists such as B. F. 12 _____ contend that Sheila and Spencer learned by

13 _____ objects with words,

14 _____ other people's speech or hand signals, and

being 15 _____ with a smile for saying or signing correctly.

Linguist Noam 16 _____ agrees that children learn from their environment, but he feels that they acquire untaught words and grammar too quickly to be explained solely by

17 _____ principles.

Instead, he contends that

all languages have the same basic building blocks and that therefore there is a

18 _____ period,

and

that all children—hearing or deaf—are born with a 19 _____

_____ device.

In support of this linguist's theory,

cognitive neuroscientists have found that we learn new languages easily as a

20 _____ (young/old) person

and

that language learning grows

21 _____ (easier/ harder) with age.

Answers may be found in the Appendix at the end of this booklet.

NOTES

NOTES

REVIEW **11.1** : **What Is Intelligence?**

Retief and Ron are university friends and are discussing their future plans.

Ron says, "I have an IQ of 120." Retief points out that Ron is

1 _____ the concept of intelligence and should instead say, "My score on an intelligence test was 120."

Retief, who's been studying intelligence in his psychology textbook, continues by noting that

he agrees with historical researcher Charles

2 _____ , who suggested that there is

a 3 _____ _____ , or *g*, factor that underlies various clusters of abilities.

Knowing that Ron is a World Checkers Champion, Retief isn't sure that Ron's verbal intelligence would show up in a cluster with his truly amazing spatial abilities

if

4 _____ _____ were used on the results of his intelligence test.

Retief, on the other hand, who is a wonderful piano keyboarder,

agrees with psychologist Robert

5 _____ , who has suggested that there are three intelligences

and that

Retief's ability to produce unique sound combinations reflects his

6 _____ intelligence,

while

his friend Ron's spatial abilities would be con-sidered 7 _____ intelligence.

Their friend Sho, who also achieves a high IQ score, has decided to become a psychotherapist.

Sho has very high

8 _____ intelligence,

which

enables him to perceive, 9 _____ ,

10 _____ , and use emotions.

Answers may be found in the Appendix at the end of this booklet.

61

In 1904, the French minister of public education wanted to find an objective way of identifying children with special needs.

He asked Alfred **1** _____ to study the problem. Assuming that all children follow

2 _____ (the same/a different) course of intellectual development, he and Théodore

3 _____ devised the first intelligence test to assess learning potential.

They measured the child's **4** _____ age, defined as the

5 _____ age typical of a given level of performance.

Years later,

Lewis **6** _____ found that this test did not work well with California students and so revised it to create the

7 _____- _____ test,

which

formed the basis for William

8 _____'s intelligence quotient (IQ) formula:

9 _____ age divided by

10 _____ age, and multiply the result by 100.

Using this formula,

the average score is

11 _____ (what number?).

Because the original IQ formula

worked fairly well for **12** _____ (adults/children) but not for **13** _____ (adults/children),

today's intelligence tests instead

produce a mental ability score based on the test-taker's performance relative to the average performance of others the same **14** _____ (gender/age/socioeconomic status).

THAT'S MY BOY, MARK... HE'S 39, BUT HE'S ALREADY READING AT A 42-YEAR OLD LEVEL...

Answers may be found in the Appendix at the end of this booklet.

REVIEW 11.3: **Assessing Intelligence**

Eighteeen-year-old Sooji is designing an intelligence test

|
that will
|

predict how well her peers will fare as they go on to higher education by assessing their

1 _____ for advanced learning.

Similarities
In what way are *wool* and *cotton* alike?

Arithmetic Reasoning
If eggs cost 60 cents a dozen, what does 1 egg cost?

Vocabulary
Tell me the meaning of corrupt.

After creating the questions, Sooji must make sure the test meets the criteria of a good psychological test.

First, she administers the test to a

2 _____

sample of students, creating a pretested group against which test-takers' scores can be compared in

order to 3 _____ the test.

Next, she must be sure that the test yields consistent results, perhaps by comparing answers to odd and even questions—that it is

4 _____ .

Finally, she must be sure the test measures and predicts what it is supposed to—that it is

5 _____ .

If the test measures students' academic potential, then it

has 6 _____ validity, because it is indeed measuring the behavior of interest.

And

if the test scores later correlate with the behavior they were attempting to predict, known as the

7 _____ , then the test

has 8 _____ validity.

0.1%   2%   13.5%   34%   34%   13.5%   2%   0.1%
55   70   85   100   115   130   145
Wechsler intelligence score

If Sooji's test meets all the criteria of a good psychological test,

|

as David 9 _____ 's intelligence scale does,

the scores of any group of people who take it should form a bell-shaped pattern

called a 10 _____ curve,

with

an average score of 11 _____ . To keep that average score, Sooji must periodically

re 12 _____ the test.

And, if Sooji had first developed and administered her test 30 years ago, then

compared the scores with the scores of today's students, she'd find that they had increased,

which is called the 13 _____ effect.

NOTES

NOTES

CHAPTER 12

REVIEW 12.1 : **Hunger and Eating Behavior**

Sitting in her afternoon psychology class, Erica regrets skipping breakfast and lunch.

As a biology major, she knows that her hunger pangs, caused by

stomach 1 _____ ,

Stomach contractions

Hunger pangs

0 1 2 3 4 5 6 7 8 9 10
Time in minutes

signal increased secretion of two chemical messengers, or

2 _____ :

3 _____ from
the pancreas

and

4 _____ from
her empty stomach.

Erica is having trouble keeping her eyes open during class (even though Professor Straub is a stimulating lecturer),

because

the increased secretion from her pancreas reduces the level of her body's energy fuel,

5 _____ , in the bloodstream.

However, Erica's brain isn't sleeping through class.

In fact, her brain's 6 _____

_____ has been secreting the

hunger-triggering hormone 7 _____ ,

and so

a very hungry Erica heads home for a large bowl of pasta. She finally feels full, a sensation triggered

by activity in the brain's 8 _____

_____ ,

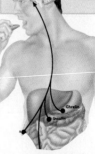

After eating, Erica weighs herself: She's 5'6" tall and weighs about 118 pounds, well below the 130-pound normal weight for her height,

but

she feels fat and, vowing to lose some weight, she takes a laxative, a clear symptom of a(n)

9 _____ _____ .

Erica's obsession with her weight has a few possible explanations:

One might be a
10 _____ (negative/positive) self-evaluation.

Or

she may have internalized and become obsessed with her Western

11 _____ 's "thin ideal."

Another possibility is that

she may be
12 _____ susceptible to eating disorders.

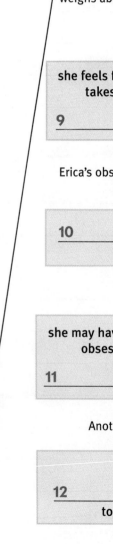

Answers may be found in the Appendix at the end of this booklet.

REVIEW 12.2: **Sexual Orientation**

Max's parents are finding it difficult to accept that he is gay.

Max explains that he 1 _____ (did/did not) choose his sexual orientation

and that he 2 _____ (can/cannot) change.

His parents want to understand why Max feels as he does, so Max begins
by discounting all the myths he's sure they've heard. Max tells them

that he does not fear the other sex, he was not

smothered by 3 _____ love or neglected by his   and that

4 _____ , he was not 5 _____
as a child,

he was not segregated by gender during

6 _____ , and he does not fear or hate

7 _____ .

Max notes that the most recent research evidence indicates

a 8 _____ basis for

one's sexual orientation.

"Fill'er up with testosterone."

For example,

researchers have found that a cell cluster in the

9 _____ and a section of the

10 _____ _____
are larger in homosexual men,

and that

between the middle of the

11 _____ (which months?) after

conception, exposure to 12 _____
levels typically experienced by a

13 _____ fetus may predispose
homosexuality in males.

Max continues to explain that

there is also evidence of a 14 _____ link: (1) homosexuality tends to run in

families, especially on the 15 _____ (mother's/father's) side;

(2) twin studies show that 16 _____ twins

are more likely than 17 _____ twins to
share a sexual orientation,

and

(3) research with fruit flies has shown that

18 _____ _____ can
determine sexual orientation.

Tonya wants to apply her knowledge of psychology in a corporate setting, so

she is taking courses in 1_____-_____ psychology. She already knows that she doesn't want to work in human factors psychology,

but now

she must decide whether she wants to help match workers to skills as a(n) 2_____ psychologist,

or

she may want to help motivate workers and improve an organization's infrastructure, as a(n) 3_____ psychologist.

Tonya must also consider which type of work

makes her feel happiest, most focused, and most involved, in other words, experience 4_____.

For example,

she may feel happiest analyzing a job, scripting questions, and training interviewers to avoid the interviewer 5_____ and perform a 6_____ interview that will pinpoint potential employees' strengths.

Or

| Percentage "satisfied" or "very satisfied" with life | 90% 80 70 60 50 40 30 20 10 0 | White collar | Manual worker | Unemployed |

she may prefer working directly with employees, focusing on their 7_____ _____ by encouraging them to attain a high standard, and attempting to increase employee 8_____ by finding ways for them to feel involved and satisfied with their work.

Part of Tonya's work in motivating employees would involve teaching managers effective management techniques. She would encourage managers to

choose an appropriate 9_____ style,

harness 10_____-_____ strengths, and

set specific, challenging 11_____.

In selecting a leadership style, managers must choose between

goal-oriented 12_____ leadership or group-oriented 13_____ leadership, and work toward managing with self-confident charisma.

They also know that

the most successful leaders tend to have a 14_____ of a goal, an ability to 15_____ it clearly, and enough optimism and faith in the group to 16_____ others.

Answers may be found in the Appendix at the end of this booklet.

NOTES

NOTES

REVIEW **13.1** ⦂ **Theories of Emotion**

Walking home from school after the basketball game, Jesse takes a shortcut through an area with no street lights. He sees a shadow of a person with something glistening in his hand, which causes him to experience the three parts of a distinct emotion.

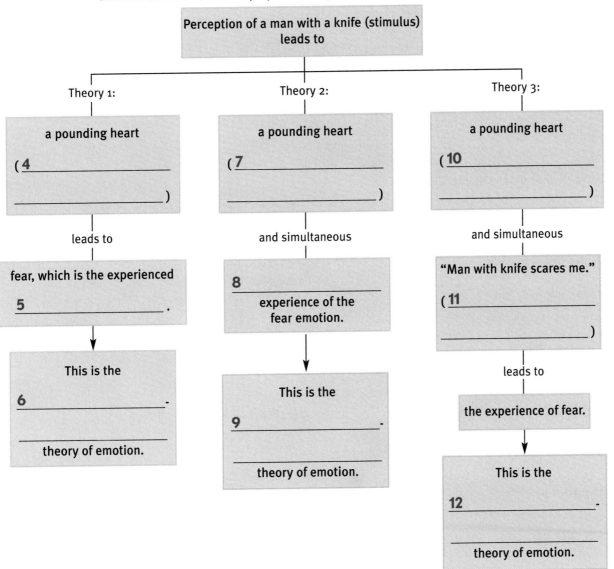

Thinking the shiny object is a knife, Jesse's heart begins to pound, which is part of his	Jesse attempts to flee, which is his	He is afraid of being stabbed, which is his
1 _____ arousal.	2 _____ behavior.	3 _____ experience of the situation.

Different theories have been proposed to explain Jesse's emotional experience.

Perception of a man with a knife (stimulus) leads to

Theory 1:	Theory 2:	Theory 3:
a pounding heart (4 _____ _____)	a pounding heart (7 _____ _____)	a pounding heart (10 _____ _____)
leads to	and simultaneous	and simultaneous
fear, which is the experienced 5 _____ .	8 _____ experience of the fear emotion.	"Man with knife scares me." (11 _____ _____)
This is the 6 _____ - _____ theory of emotion.	This is the 9 _____ - _____ theory of emotion.	leads to
		the experience of fear.
		This is the 12 _____ - _____ theory of emotion.

Answers may be found in the Appendix at the end of this booklet.

71

REVIEW 13.2: Embodied Emotion

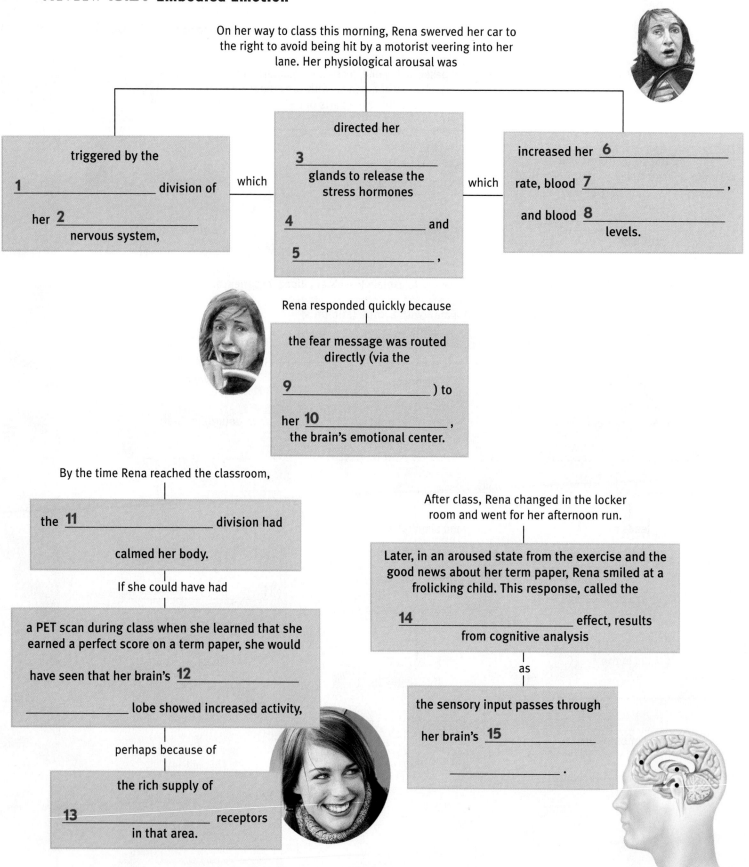

On her way to class this morning, Rena swerved her car to the right to avoid being hit by a motorist veering into her lane. Her physiological arousal was

triggered by the

1 _____ division of

her 2 _____

nervous system,

which

directed her

3 _____

glands to release the stress hormones

4 _____ and

5 _____ ,

which

increased her 6 _____

rate, blood 7 _____ ,

and blood 8 _____

levels.

Rena responded quickly because

the fear message was routed directly (via the

9 _____) to

her 10 _____ ,

the brain's emotional center.

By the time Rena reached the classroom,

the 11 _____ division had

calmed her body.

If she could have had

a PET scan during class when she learned that she earned a perfect score on a term paper, she would

have seen that her brain's 12 _____

_____ lobe showed increased activity,

perhaps because of

the rich supply of

13 _____ receptors

in that area.

After class, Rena changed in the locker room and went for her afternoon run.

Later, in an aroused state from the exercise and the good news about her term paper, Rena smiled at a frolicking child. This response, called the

14 _____ effect, results

from cognitive analysis

as

the sensory input passes through

her brain's 15 _____

_____ .

72   Answers may be found in the Appendix at the end of this booklet.

Alycia is in a good mood because she just learned that a good friend is coming to visit tomorrow. On her way home, she sees an infant drop her pacifier. Alycia picks it up

> cheerfully for the young mother, a reflection of the
>
> 1_____-_____, _____-_____ phenomenon.

As she is walking home, Alycia thinks: "I'm pretty lucky— I'm young and healthy, and I have lots of close friends. And I have a $1000 scholarship to the university of my choice."

> Researchers in the new field of 2_____ psychology would say that her life satisfaction, or
>
> 3_____ well-being, is high.

A few days later, Alycia learns that her friend Lois has received a scholarship that will pay all her higher education tuition.

> Comparing her meager scholarship to Lois' full scholarship reduces Alycia's satisfaction,
>
> producing in her a sense of 4_____
>
> _____ .

Importance scores vs. Life satisfaction graph, showing lines for Money and Love.

Being a generally positive person, however,

with

> a more active 5_____
>
> _____ lobe in her brain

and

> high 6_____-_____ , Alycia judges her current financial status against her prior financial problems

and

> feels content, which psychologists refer to as the
>
> 7_____-_____ phenomenon.

NOTES

NOTES

CHAPTER 14

REVIEW 14.1 : **Stress and the Body's Responses**

Instead of studying, Jennifer went out with her friends last night, so she's poorly prepared for today's biology exam. Her level of stress is high because

she is thinking about, or 1_____ , this particular

2_____ , or test, as beyond her coping abilities.

Jennifer's response was first described by

Walter 3_____ and later
refined by physiologists who identified a

4_____-_____ system,

in which

the 5_____ nervous system

directs the 6_____ glands

to

release the stress hormones 7_____

and 8_____ .

These hormones are responsible for Jennifer's

9_____ (immediate/sustained)
response to stress.

At the same time, the brain's

10_____ _____ , by way of the

11_____ and the pituitary gland,

directs the 12_____ glands to

release the 13_____ stress

hormones, such as 14_____ .

These hormones are responsible for Jennifer's

15_____ (immediate/sustained) response
to stress.

When stressed, Jennifer's autonomic nervous system (ANS) does not distinguish between a difficult test and an attacking lion. Either way, the ANS responds by

increasing her 16_____ rate and
respiration, diverting blood from digestion to her

skeletal 17_____ ,

and

releasing sugar and fat to prepare her body for

18_____ or 19_____ .

(Continued on the next page.)

Driving home after class, Jennifer notices her car is overheating, then sees flames bursting from under the hood. In response to this new stressor,

her heart begins to beat wildly and she feels faint, what

Hans 20 _____ called the alarm

reaction or the 21 _____

_____ syndrome.

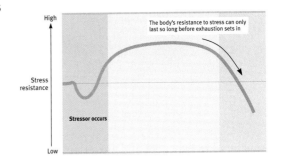

High

The body's resistance to stress can only last so long before exhaustion sets in

Stress resistance

Stressor occurs

Low

In the second phase of the syndrome,

called 22 _____ , she swerves over to the side of the road and leaps out of her car.

The firefighters who extinguish the flames also comfort Jennifer, but

the combined stresses of the day have led her to the third stage,

23 _____ .

A few days later, Jennifer comes down with a wicked cold, which

might be an effect of the stress weakening her

24 _____ system, including

the activity of the 25 _____

and 26 _____ .

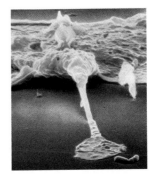

Immune system in action

Malcolm has been trying to quit smoking for years, but it's very difficult.

SNAPSHOTS at jasonlove.com

He started smoking during early

1 _____ for two main reasons:

He wanted to look cool and grown-up, so he

2 _____ his behavior after admired actors he'd seen smoking in movies,

and

he felt pressured by his 3 _____ who were already smoking.

Today, 20 years later, Malcolm has tried several techniques for quitting (the patch, gum, etc.), but nothing works because

he is 4 _____ on nicotine. In fact, he now needs two packs instead of one to get the same effect, because he has developed a

5 _____ for the drug.

Malcolm's addiction is due to several factors:

First, nicotine triggers the release of

6 _____ and

7 _____ ,

which

boosts 8 _____ and mental efficiency, abilities that Malcolm feels are important for his work.

Second, nicotine stimulates the central nervous system to release

9 _____

that

calm 10 _____ and reduce sensitivity to

11 _____ .

To make matters worse, Malcolm's family and friends,

almost all of whom smoke, 12 _____ (will/will not) support his efforts by quitting with him.

Answers may be found in the Appendix at the end of this booklet.

NOTES

NOTES

REVIEW **15.1** : **The Psychoanalytic Perspective**

Klaus is 18 years old and, like all adolescents,
he is trying to figure out who he is.

He wants to know why he thinks, feels, and acts the way he
does; that is, he wants to define his **1**_____ .

Klaus decides to read about the various personality
theorists, beginning with

Sigmund **2**_____ , who believed that
most of the mind is hidden from view and therefore
3_____ ,

and that

personality is a product of the **4**_____
between our basic sexual and aggressive impulses,

directed by the **5**_____ , and social restraint

derived from the **6**_____ .

After reading about this psychoanalytic theory,
Klaus decided that his long-standing aggressive
behavior toward his younger brother

could have been the result of

7_____ his anger with his
parents for being so strict.

This

would protect him from the
8_____ he might feel
if he were to express that anger.

Perhaps

the part of his personality called the

9_____ redirects his anger, and so

the hitting of his brother is a **10**_____

mechanism called **11**_____ .

Klaus also thought that he may have **12**_____ his behavior
by saying that his brother needed the discipline.

Answers may be found in the Appendix at the end of this booklet.

81

Klaus isn't sure he agrees with Freud's theory. Klaus thinks that

Freud placed too much emphasis on the

1 _____ mind and on sex and

2 _____ as all-consuming motives.

Instead,

Klaus thinks he is more likely to be guided

by his **3** _____ mind, though he

still believes that **4** _____
interactions had a great effect on his behavior.

Klaus learns that his beliefs match the neo-Freudian movement. The neo-Freudians emphasized different aspects of personality.

Alfred **5** _____
emphasized peoples' efforts to
overcome feelings of

6 _____ .

Karen **7** _____
believed that childhood

8 _____ triggers our
desire for love and security.

Unlike the others, Carl

9 _____ agreed
with Freud's notion of a(n)

10 _____

but

thought it was more of a

11 _____
unconscious that included images
derived from our species' history.

Klaus wonders, though, if

the modern psychoanalysts—those who profess a

12 _____ approach—aren't closer to
having a true understanding of personalty. He knows

that

they **13** _____ (agree/disagree) with
Freud's overall personality structure and his

classifying people as oral, **14** _____ ,

or _____ ,

but

they respect the reality that many of our
day-to-day thought processes are indeed

15 _____ .

REVIEW 15.3: The Trait Perspective

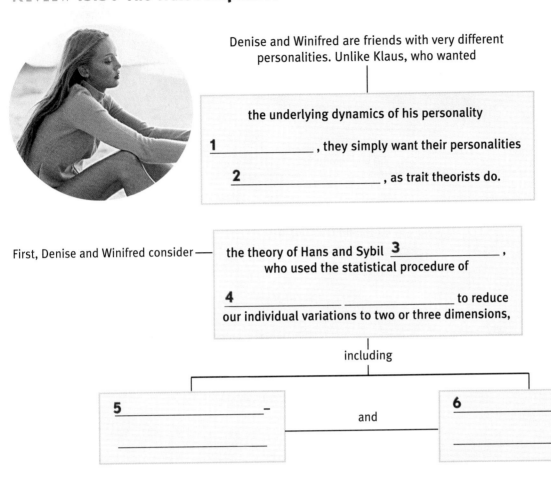

Denise and Winifred are friends with very different personalities. Unlike Klaus, who wanted

the underlying dynamics of his personality

1 _____ , they simply want their personalities

2 _____ , as trait theorists do.

First, Denise and Winifred consider ——

the theory of Hans and Sybil **3** _____ , who used the statistical procedure of

4 _____ _____ to reduce our individual variations to two or three dimensions,

including

5 _____ – _____

and

6 _____ – _____ .

Denise tends to be

quiet, reserved, thoughtful, and calm, so she is more likely to be classified as

7 _____ and **8** _____ .

Winifred, on the other hand, is

outgoing, lively, restless, and impulsive, so she is more likely to be classified as

9 _____ and **10** _____ .

Winifred and Denise decide to volunteer for neuroscience research on personality in order to learn more. They find evidence that their personalities have a biological basis.

For example, they learn that the areas of Winifred's

11 _____ _____ involved in behavior inhibition are less active than the same areas in Denise's brain.

They also

learn that their **12** _____ played a significant role in creating their

13 _____ , which helped define their personalities.

(Continued on the next page.)

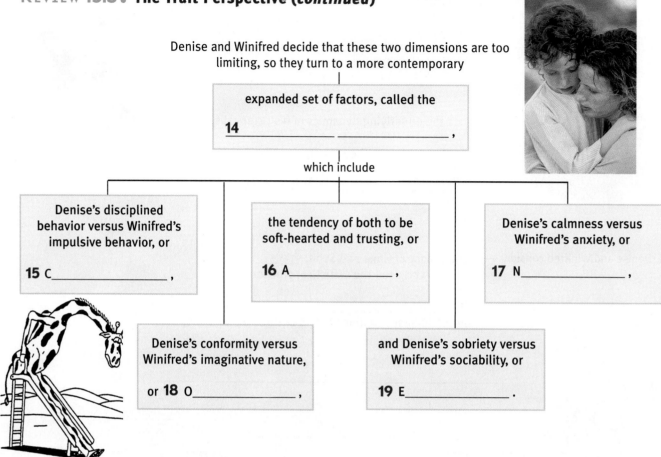

Denise and Winifred decide that these two dimensions are too limiting, so they turn to a more contemporary

expanded set of factors, called the

14 _____ _____ ,

which include

Denise's disciplined behavior versus Winifred's impulsive behavior, or

15 C _____ ,

the tendency of both to be soft-hearted and trusting, or

16 A _____ ,

Denise's calmness versus Winifred's anxiety, or

17 N _____ ,

Denise's conformity versus Winifred's imaginative nature,

or **18** O _____ ,

and Denise's sobriety versus Winifred's sociability, or

19 E _____ .

Checking the research, Denise and Winifred find evidence that

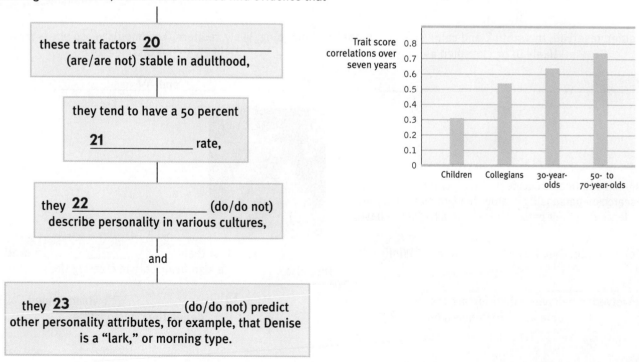

these trait factors **20** _____ (are/are not) stable in adulthood,

they tend to have a 50 percent

21 _____ rate,

they **22** _____ (do/do not) describe personality in various cultures,

and

they **23** _____ (do/do not) predict other personality attributes, for example, that Denise is a "lark," or morning type.

Trait score correlations over seven years

0.8
0.7
0.6
0.5
0.4
0.3
0.2
0.1
0

Children   Collegians   30-year-olds   50- to 70-year-olds

Answers may be found in the Appendix at the end of this booklet.

Denise and Winifred can't stop thinking about how their personalities are formed. Knowing that

psychological science views people as

1 bio_____ organisms, they set their sights

on Albert **2**_____'s theory.

This theorist

emphasizes the interaction of internal

3_____ factors,

4_____ , and the environment,

a process he called **5**_____

_____ .

The interaction varies between Denise and Winifred for several possible reasons, including the following:

They choose different
6_____ :
Denise might choose to go to the library, while Winifred chooses a coffee shop with friends.

Their internal thoughts, or
7_____ , shape how they interpret and react to events: Denise takes challenges in stride, while Winifred becomes anxious.

Their **8**_____ create the situations to which they react: Denise shies away from people, while Winifred greets them warmly.

According to this theory, how Denise and Winifred react to their environment depends on certain factors, including

their sense of **9**_____

_____ (hint: internal or external)

and

their attributional style (**10**_____

or **11**_____).

"We just haven't been flapping them hard enough."

Finally, both Denise and Winifred learn the importance of maintaining a positive attitude and building on their strengths,

based on the research of Martin

12_____ , which indicates that optimal human functioning benefits health.

NOTES

NOTES

CHAPTER 16

REVIEW 16.1 : Anxiety Disorders

Carol almost constantly feels extremely tense and uneasy for no apparent reason. She cannot concentrate on her studies, and she's on the verge of failing all her courses. This suggests that

| she may suffer from a
| 1 _____
|
| _____ disorder,

which

| may lead to
| 2 _____
| problems, such as ulcers and high blood pressure.

Because Carol cannot identify the cause of her tension,

| it would be described by Sigmund
| 3 _____ as
| 4 _____ - _____ ,

while

| learning theorists would link her anxiety with
| 5 _____ _____
| of fear, and biological psychologists might link it to an
| overarousal of 6 _____ areas
| involved in 7 _____ control.

Carol's roommate Shayna complains of similar feelings but also

| experiences unexpected episodes of intense dread, known as
| 8 _____ attacks,

which

| are accompanied by physical symptoms such as
| heart 9 _____ , shortness of breath, and choking sensations.

Shayna has experienced several of these frightening episodes and has begun to avoid situations in which

| she fears 10 _____
| may be difficult.

Thus,

| Shayna is developing a fear of leaving her home, which may become
| 11 _____ if the feelings intensify.

Carol and Shayna's friend Randal doesn't understand their inability to identify the source of their anxiety. He says,

| "I know exactly what I fear: heights.
| I have a 12 _____ ,

which

| I know is 13 _____ ,
| but at least I can deal with it by avoiding tall buildings, for example.

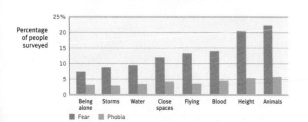

| I believe I 14 _____ my fear from my dad, after watching him fall off our roof and never climbing a ladder again."

Percentage of people surveyed
25%
20
15
10
5
0

Being alone | Storms | Water | Close spaces | Flying | Blood | Height | Animals

■ Fear ■ Phobia

(Continued on the next page.)

While Randal is talking with Carol and Shayna, another friend Moira is making her third trip to the restroom to wash her hands.

Moira has become 15 _____ with the idea that doorknobs or any objects handled by others are full of germs. By giving in to her

16 _____ to wash her hands, she thinks she eliminates the germs. But this constant hand-washing is interfering with her everyday life.

One useful explanation for Moira's behavior is biological: Brain scans have shown that an area that monitors our actions and checks for errors, the 17 _____

_____ cortex, is especially likely to be hyperactive in people with Moira's disorder.

Alternatively,

learning theorists would say that actions such as frequent hand-washing reduce a sufferer's

18 _____ , thus reinforcing the hand-washing.

As they talk, the four friends remember Shayna's brother Shawn, who is an Army lieutenant serving in Afghanistan. In his many e-mails, he has described to Shayna some horrific situations. Shayna fears that

when Shawn returns, he will have nightmares and suffer other constant reminders of the horrors he has seen, which would be symptoms of

19 _____-_____

_____ disorder.

As explained by

20 _____ theorists, any reminders of

his war-time experiences will bring out feelings of

21 _____ .

REVIEW 16.2: Mood Disorders

Dwayne's parents (Isabel and Max) are worried about him. Dwayne's fiancée Arlene recently died in a car accident and since then

Dwayne has been lethargic and has lost all interest in family and friends. This behavior has lasted for more than two weeks, suggesting that he is suffering from

1 _____ _____ disorder,

which

is more common in

2 _____ (men/women)

than in 3 _____ (men/women).

Isabel and Max think there may be a biological explanation for Dwayne's condition. They

recall that Isabel's mother and sister were both diagnosed with psychological problems, indicating a

4 _____ influence.

However,

a psychologist with a social-

5 _____ perspective suggests that

Dwayne's 6 _____-_____ beliefs

and

7 _____ explanatory style may also be contributing to his inability to get over the loss of his fiancée.

After about a month, Dwayne comes out of his room, all excited with plans to move to Hawaii and start a new career in real estate.

Max and Isabel's psychologist suggests that these symptoms may indicate the

presence of 8 _____ disorder, which is characterized by alternating mood

swings between 9 _____ and

the overexcited state of 10 _____ .

Depressed state
(May 17)

Manic state
(May 18)

Depressed state
(May 27)

Researchers have found that during bipolar episodes of depression, brain levels of

11 _____ and

12 _____ are low,

and

one of these neurotransmitters,

13 _____ , is overabundant

during bipolar episodes of mania.

Answers may be found in the Appendix at the end of this booklet.

REVIEW 16.3: Schizophrenia

The Swiss Guards are blocking his way, but Trevor insists that he be let in: "I am the Pope," he says.

Trevor is experiencing a 1 _____ ,

which is a common symptom of 2 _____ .

Other symptoms include the following:

The voices Trevor hears that tell him he is Pope and that he must "say the Mass this morning"

are auditory 3 _____ .

Trevor also laughs hysterically when the Guard points a gun at him, thus exhibiting

4 _____ emotions.

Given the presence of odd behaviors, Trevor's symptoms are considered

5 _____ (positive/negative), and they seem to indicate that he

has 6 _____ schizophrenia.

Red areas show tissue loss in adolescents with schizophrenia.

Trevor has been in and out of psychiatric hospitals since he was a teenager, indicating that

he suffers from 7 _____ , or process, schizophrenia

and that

his chances of recovery are

8 _____ (good/poor).

Enlarged cranial cavity in person with schizophrenia.

Researchers have proposed several explanations for schizophrenia.

One explanation involves low brain activity in the

9 _____ _____
and a noticeable decline in the brain waves that reflect

10 _____ neural firing.

An alternative explanation suggests that a midpregnancy

11 _____ infection impairs brain development in the fetus.

Schizophrenia is largely influenced by genetic and biochemical factors, but extreme stress often triggers the disorder, which indicates that

12 _____ also plays a role in its onset.

Answers may be found in the Appendix at the end of this booklet.

NOTES

NOTES

CHAPTER 17

REVIEW 17.1 : Psychoanalysis

At his friends' urging, Barney has decided to seek help for the depression he has been been struggling with ever since moving away from home and starting college two months ago. He's heard a lot about

Sigmund 1_____'s therapy, called

2_____ ,

in which

patients use 3_____

_____ to express
whatever comes to mind

in order to

uncover their 4_____

unconscious conflicts.

In this therapy,

analysts traditionally would interpret their
patients' tendency to change the subject
in response to difficult questions

as 5_____ ,

and

if a patient's anger toward abusive family
members began to be directed at the therapist,
that defense would be interpreted as

6_____ .

Barney finds, however, that this therapy is practiced by
only a very few therapists and that most are instead

offering an updated version called

7_____ therapy.

In this therapy,

current symptoms are analyzed to consider themes

across important 8_____ ,
such as those between Barney and his family
members back home.

Or,

Barney might be helped best by the brief

variation known as 9_____ psychotherapy,

which

may enable him to gain 10_____
into the root of his problem.

Answers may be found in the Appendix at the end of this booklet.

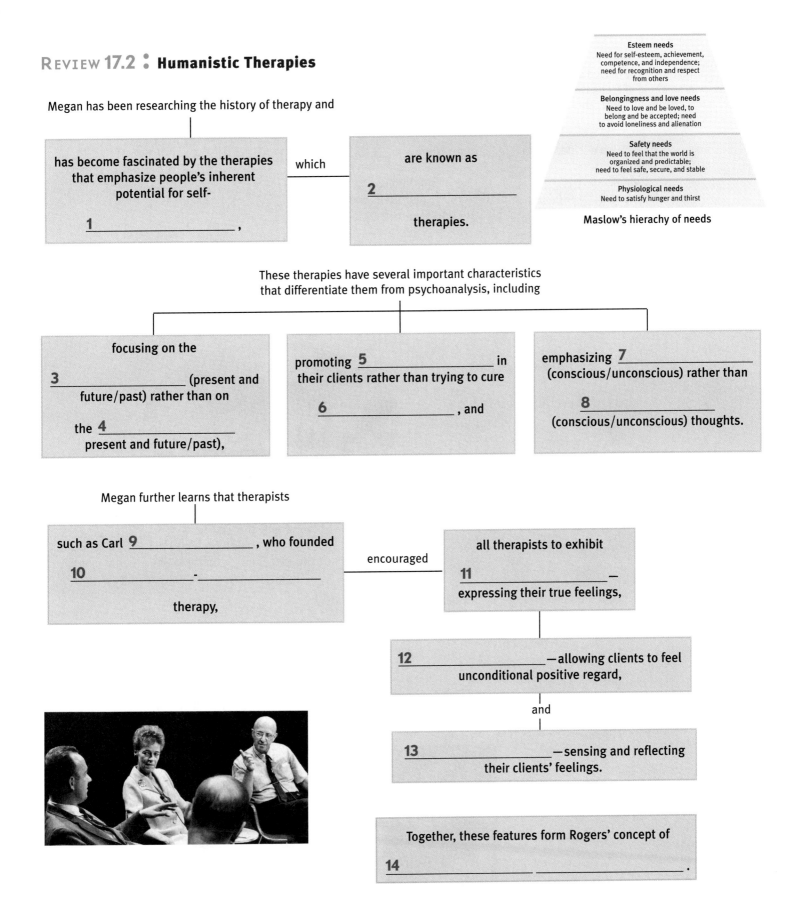

REVIEW **17.2** ⦂ **Humanistic Therapies**

Megan has been researching the history of therapy and

has become fascinated by the therapies that emphasize people's inherent potential for self-

1 _____ ,

which

are known as

2 _____

therapies.

Esteem needs
Need for self-esteem, achievement, competence, and independence; need for recognition and respect from others

Belongingness and love needs
Need to love and be loved, to belong and be accepted; need to avoid loneliness and alienation

Safety needs
Need to feel that the world is organized and predictable; need to feel safe, secure, and stable

Physiological needs
Need to satisfy hunger and thirst

Maslow's hierachy of needs

These therapies have several important characteristics that differentiate them from psychoanalysis, including

focusing on the

3 _____ (present and future/past) rather than on

the **4** _____ present and future/past),

promoting **5** _____ in their clients rather than trying to cure

6 _____ , and

emphasizing **7** _____ (conscious/unconscious) rather than

8 _____ (conscious/unconscious) thoughts.

Megan further learns that therapists

such as Carl **9** _____ , who founded

10 _____-_____ therapy,

encouraged

all therapists to exhibit

11 _____—expressing their true feelings,

12 _____—allowing clients to feel unconditional positive regard,

and

13 _____—sensing and reflecting their clients' feelings.

Together, these features form Rogers' concept of

14 _____ _____ .

REVIEW 17.3: **Behavior Therapies**

Trish recently moved across Canada for her studies, but she
is so afraid of flying that she now rarely sees her family and
friends at home. This fear is interfering with her life, so

Trish decides to seek help from a therapist

who uses **1**_____ conditioning
principles to pair the stimulus that triggers her fear (flying) with
a new response that is incompatible with that fear (relaxation),

which is referred to as

2_____ .

The therapist proposes

a technique called systematic

3_____ ,

which is

a type of **4**_____ therapy that

pairs **5**_____

with

gradually increasing **6**_____-
triggering stimuli (going to the airport, going to
the gate, getting on the plane, learning about
flight procedures, actually taking a flight).

However, Trish is embarrassed by the idea of
exposing her fears in public (at the airport).

So,

the therapist suggests **7**_____
_____ exposure therapy,

which

would allow Trish to work through her fears by
way of vivid, three-dimensional, computer

8_____ .

Answers may be found in the Appendix at the end of this booklet.

REVIEW 17.4 : Cognitive Therapy for Depression

Lola is searching for a therapist. After her mother and father divorced and he moved away, she began reading about cognitive therapies, hoping those reading about techniques might help her get on with her life.

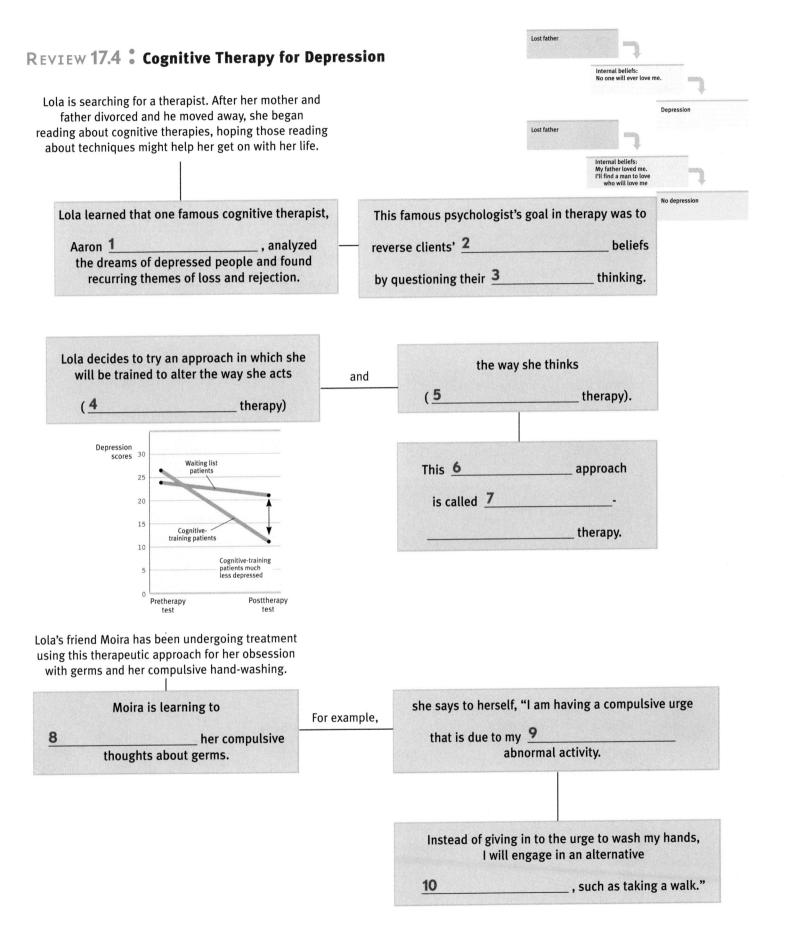

Lost father

Internal beliefs:
No one will ever love me.

Depression

Lost father

Internal beliefs:
My father loved me.
I'll find a man to love who will love me

No depression

Lola learned that one famous cognitive therapist, Aaron **1** _____ , analyzed the dreams of depressed people and found recurring themes of loss and rejection.

This famous psychologist's goal in therapy was to reverse clients' **2** _____ beliefs by questioning their **3** _____ thinking.

Lola decides to try an approach in which she will be trained to alter the way she acts (**4** _____ therapy)

and

the way she thinks (**5** _____ therapy).

This **6** _____ approach is called **7** _____-_____ therapy.

Depression scores

Waiting list patients

Cognitive-training patients

Cognitive-training patients much less depressed

Pretherapy test

Posttherapy test

Lola's friend Moira has been undergoing treatment using this therapeutic approach for her obsession with germs and her compulsive hand-washing.

Moira is learning to **8** _____ her compulsive thoughts about germs.

For example,

she says to herself, "I am having a compulsive urge that is due to my **9** _____ abnormal activity.

Instead of giving in to the urge to wash my hands, I will engage in an alternative **10** _____ , such as taking a walk."

Jessica's therapist has diagnosed her with major depressive disorder and has suggested that her recovery may be expedited if

she takes an

1 _____ drug such as Prozac.

Because

her therapist is a 2 _____ , he can prescribe drugs to his patients.

Unlike the 3 _____ drugs, which depress central nervous system activity,

these drugs

work by increasing the availability of

4 _____ or

5 _____ ,

which

Message is sent across synaptic gap.

Message is received; excess neurotransmitter molecules are reabsorbed by sending neuron.

Prozac partially blocks normal reuptake of the neurotransmitter serotonin; excess serotonin in synapse enhances its mood-lifting effect.

Sending neuron
Vesicles containing neurotransmitters
Action potential
Synaptic gap
Neurotransmitter molecule
Receptors
Receiving neuron
Reuptake
Serotonin
Prozac

are neurotransmitters that elevate

6 _____ and arousal and

are 7 _____ (scarce/plentiful) in depression.

Prozac is called a 8 _____ - _____ - inhibitor (SSRI)

because

it partially blocks the reabsorption

of 9 _____

from neural 10 _____ .

If the drugs and psychotherapy together don't work for Jessica, her therapist may suggest the most controversial treatment for depression,

11 _____ _____ , which involves sending a brief electrical current through the patient's brain.

stimulating electrodes
recording EEG
ground
recording
ECT device
blood pressure cuff monitor
blood pressure cuff for EMG
EMG

Alternatively,

Wire coil
Pulsed magnetic field
Positioning frame
Activated neurons
Resting neurons

Jessica might try 12 _____ _____ stimulation (rTMS), which produces fewer side effects such as 13 _____ or 14 _____ loss.

Answers may be found in the Appendix at the end of this booklet.

NOTES

NOTES

Aimee sees Monica—a girl from her class whom she doesn't know except by name—running out of a jewelry store. Aimee thinks, "She must have stolen something and is running away."

Aimee shares that suspicion with some friends.

Aimee is 1 _____ Monica's

behavior to her 2 _____ .

In fact, Monica got a phone call saying that her Mom had been rushed to the hospital, and she was racing to meet her there.

Her behavior was actually due to the

3 _____ ,

and so

Aimee had made the 4 _____

_____ error .

The idea that people usually attribute others' behavior either to their

5 _____ dispositions or to their 6 _____

situations was proposed by Fritz 7 _____ .

Because Aimee's incorrect beliefs about Monica are negative,

she is predisposed to develop a negative

8 _____ toward Monica
and to behave accordingly if

other influences are

9 _____
(strong/minimal),

her attitude is

10 _____
(specific/not specific) to the behavior,

and she is keenly

11 _____
of her feelings.

she experiences 12 _____

_____ , because her new
understanding now conflicts with her past behaviors.

When Aimee learns the truth about Monica's behavior,

Answers may be found in the Appendix at the end of this booklet.

101

Calvin does not belong to a fraternity. His friend Theo has pledged with Omega Psi. Although they once were close,

they have drifted apart because Theo is

1 _____ his thinking and behavior to the standards set by his fraternity brothers.

Research by Solomon 2 _____

identified factors that may have contributed to Theo's changed behavior, including the following:

Theo was made to feel

3 _____ by upper-classmen when he was pledging.

The other Omega Psi fraternity brothers were

4 _____ in their views.

Theo 5 _____ Omega Psi's status and attractiveness on campus.

Changing his behavior in order to gain his fraternity brothers' approval meant that Theo was succumbing

to 6 _____ social influence.

David, the president of Theo's fraternity, has ordered all pledges to befriend only fellow fraternity brothers.

Because David is considered a

legitimate 7 _____ figure,

Theo obeys his order. As Stanley

8 _____'s research results would predict, Theo refuses to associate with Calvin, who does not belong to his fraternity.

Theo's fraternity sets the social 9 _____ for brothers' behavior, and not one brother veers from the rules, so

there are no 10 _____

_____ for defiance.

Answers may be found in the Appendix at the end of this booklet.

Two new biology majors, Wynona and Jason, have been hired as work-study students in the lab.

The amount of time they spend in close
1 _____ is a powerful predictor
that they will at least develop a friendship.

As the days and months go by,
their liking for each other

will most likely increase. This is because of
the 2 _____
_____ effect,

which

according to 3 _____
psychologists is adaptive; our ancestors
survived because they found that what was
different was potentially dangerous, and what
was 4 _____ was safe.

Wynona and Jason also find each other
5 _____ , which
contributes to their budding relationship.

RUBES® By Leigh Rubin

Wynona and Jason begin dating and, as
they get to know each other,

their liking increases because they
6 _____ (share/do not share)
interests and values.

Also,

because they both feel that the benefits of
their relationship outweigh the costs, the
7 _____ theory predicts
that the relationship will grow and develop.

Using the 8 _____-
_____ theory of
emotion to explain what has now become
passionate love between Jason and Wynona,

Elaine 9 _____ would
identify the ingredients of their love as

physical 10 _____ and
cognitive 11 _____ .

With time, their passionate love may
develop into 12 _____
love, which is characterized

by

equal giving and receiving
by both partners, or
13 _____ ,

and by

both revealing their dreams
and worries, or self-
14 _____ .

NOTES

NOTES

Answers Appendix

PROLOGUE
The Story of Psychology

Review P.1: Prescientific Psychology

The ancient Greek philosopher **(1) Socrates** and his student **(2) Plato** argued that the **(3) mind** is separable from the **(4) body.** These philosophers derived their principles by **(5) logic,** while Plato's student **(6) Aristotle** emphasized the importance of careful **(7) observation** and the idea that knowledge springs from **(8) experiences** stored in **(9) memory.** In the seventeenth century, the French philosopher René **(10) Descartes,** in order to explain how mind and body communicated, concluded that the fluid in the brain contained **(11) animal spirits,** which flowed through nerve paths and enabled simple behaviors called **(12) reflexes.** Meanwhile, the English scientists Francis Bacon and John **(13) Locke** proposed the view that knowledge originates in **(14) experience,** which is the basis for modern **(15) functionalism.**

Review P.2: Contemporary Psychology

Psychology as we know it began in a laboratory in Germany in the year **(1) 1879,** when Wilhelm **(2) Wundt** tried to measure simple **(3) mental** processes. His student Edward **(4) Titchener** established the school of psychology called **(5) structuralism,** which aimed to discover the elements of the mind. He used the method known as **(6) introspection,** which involved asking people to look inward. This method proved to be **(7) unreliable.** At the same time, another American, William **(8) James,** focused on how **(9) mental** and **(10) behavioral** processes enable the human species to survive, establishing the school of psychology called **(11) empiricism.** Beginning in the 1920s, while Wundt, Titchener, and James engaged in the study of **(12) internal** life—our inner sensations, images and feelings—American psychologists led by John **(13) Watson** and then by B. F. **(14) Skinner** redefined psychology as the scientific study of **(15) observable behavior.** In the 1960s, a softer response to this "mechanistic" view, **(16) humanistic** psychology, was pioneered by Carl Rogers and Abraham Maslow. Today, with reinvigorated interest in inner thoughts and feelings, psychology is defined as the science of **(17) behavior** and **(18) mental** processes.

Review P.3: Levels of Analysis

As complex individuals with widely varying behavior, we are part of a larger **(1) social** system but also composed of smaller **(2) physical** subsystems. This suggests three main levels of analysis of our **(3) behavior** and **(4) mental** processes, which together form an integrated **(5) biopsychosocial** approach that incorporates **(6) biological** influences, **(7) psychological** influences, and **(8) social-cultural** influences.

For example, to better understand why a person is generally happy, a psychologist working from the

- neuroscience perspective might consider how particular **(9) brain** circuits control the person's emotions.
- evolutionary perspective might consider how optimism (a trait of happy people) facilitated the survival of our ancestors' **(10) genes.**
- behavior genetics perspective might consider how **(11) heredity** and **(12) environment** influence temperament.
- psychodynamic perspective might consider how recognizing and resolving **(13) unconscious** childhood conflicts could lead to a feeling of satisfaction.

- behavioral perspective might consider how the person **(14) learns** positive responses to certain stimuli.
- cognitive perspective might consider how information is encoded, processed, stored, and **(15) retrieved** so that it leads to upbeat thoughts.
- social-cultural perspective might consider how behavior has been affected by specific **(16) situations** and by more general **(17) environmental influences.**

The important point is that the different perspectives **(18) complement** one another.

Chapter 1
Thinking Critically With Psychological Science

Review 1.1: Science Versus Intuition

Our feelings of intuition and common sense are notoriously **(1) inaccurate** and limited because of certain tendencies. For example, after you hear that two friends are splitting up as a couple, you say it was inevitable, because you **(2) knew all along** they were wrong for each other, a tendency called **(3) hindsight bias.** As another example, when your Aunt Betty is so sure she can find her way to a new friend's house that her quick right turn nearly lands her in the ocean, she is exhibiting **(4) overconfidence.** To counteract these tendencies to overvalue intuition, researchers rely on a **(5) scientific attitude** to examine **(6) assumptions** (Is the rumor true?), discern hidden **(7) values** (Might you have been jealous of your friends?), evaluate **(8) evidence** (The couple hasn't been seen together recently), and assess **(9) conclusions** (These two are no longer a pair). This attitude is also called **(10) critical** thinking.

Review 1.2: The Scientific Method

Dr. Windham contends that contact between people of different ethnicities and cultures increases liking. Using the scientific method, he develops a scientific **(1) theory** that enables him to **(2) organize** relevant observations, such as different groups choosing to have lunch together, and interpret the meaning of those observations. The set of principles Dr. Windham has developed generates testable **(3) predictions** called **(4) hypotheses**—for example, that people with such contact score lower on an ingroup bias scale. Dr. Windham then conducts **(5) research**—for example, administering tests to measure degree of bias before and after contact. From the results, he accepts, **(6) rejects,** or **(7) revises** his hypothesis. Dr. Windham reports his findings with precise **(8) operational definitions** of concepts that allow others to **(9) replicate** his research.

Review 1.3: Research Methods

Dr. Alvarez wants to study increased suicide rates among teenagers. She develops a hypothesis that anxiety leads to depression, which may lead to suicidal behavior. She has a variety of research methods to choose from. She can focus on one or two extreme situations to educate herself about depression among young people, a method called the **(1) case study,** which can suggest **(2) hypotheses** for further study, but the information generated may not be **(3) representative** of all young people. Dr. Alvarez could also conduct a **(4) survey,** interviewing **(5) many** teenagers in **(6) less** depth, creating questions carefully to avoid **(7) wording** effects. If Dr. Alvarez were to interview only depressed teens and then assume that most teens are depressed, she would be experiencing a phenomenon called the **(8) false consensus** effect. Instead, Dr. Alvarez will study a **(9) random sample** of the teen population, ensuring that they are **(10) representative** of all teens. Yet another alternative would be for Dr. Alvarez to study teenagers at school or at play, a method called **(11) naturalistic** observation. However, none of the three **(12) research** methods included on this page actually **(13) explains** why a behavior happens.

Describing behavior is a first step toward **(14) predicting** it. If Dr. Alvarez finds that two traits occur together—as anxiety increases, so does depression—she can say that they are positively **(15) correlated,** and she can express this relationship in the form of a **(16) scatterplot.** To determine whether anxiety **(17) causes** depression, Dr. Alvarez conducts an **(18) experiment,** randomly assigning participants to two groups—teens who are exposed to an anxiety-arousing movie, the **(19) experimental** group, and teens who see a romantic movie, the **(20) control** group. Both groups then take a test to measure depression. In this study, the movie is the **(21) independent** variable—the variable that is manipulated in order to see the effect on the teens' level of depression, which is the **(22) dependent** variable.

Chapter 2
Neuroscience and Behavior

Review 2.1: Neural Communication

As Shay drives down the street, approaching a major intersection, the traffic signal changes to red. For her to perceive the change, light is transmitted to the backs of her eyes, where **(1) sensory** neurons can be activated. This information is received on branching fibers called **(2) dendrites.** When the signal reaches the cell body, if the **(3) excitatory** signals minus the **(4) inhibitory** signals exceed the neuron's **(5) threshold,** gates on the neuron's **(6) axon** open and allow **(7) positively** charged atoms to enter and **(8) depolarize** that part of the membrane. The resulting **(9) action potential** travels down the axon, which is often coated with an insulating sheath of **(10) myelin** that increases the speed of transmission. When the signal reaches the end of the axon, chemicals called **(11) neurotransmitters** are released into the **(12) synaptic** gap between the **(13) sending** and the **(14) receiving** neurons.

Review 2.2: The Nervous System

The neural message about the traffic signal travels from Shay's eyes via the **(1) somatic** division of her **(2) peripheral** nervous system and is routed by the brain's sensory switchboard, the **(3) thalamus,** to the **(4) occipital** lobes of her **(5) cerebral cortex.** When the information about the traffic light reaches Shay's brain, it is processed by **(6) interneurons** in uncommitted areas of tissue, called **(7) association** areas, which belong to the **(8) central** nervous system. For Shay to stop the car, her brain must send instructions to her right leg muscles via **(9) motor** neurons that cause her foot to press on the brake. If Shay notices that she's about to be cut off by another driver, the **(10) reticular formation** of her brainstem increases her level of **(11) arousal,** which causes the **(12) sympathetic** division of her **(13) autonomic** nervous system to trigger bodily changes that help meet the emergency, such as accelerated **(14) heartbeat,** elevated blood **(15) sugar,** and slowing of **(16) digestion.** After the emergency, Shay's body is restored to its pre-emergency state by the **(17) parasympathetic** nervous system.

Review 2.3: The Brain

Dave Matthews, the guitarist, is able to play the guitar through the activity of many parts of his brain. Information is routed from Matthews' eyes, ears, and fingertips via the **(1) thalamus** to the upper-level brain structures: **(2) motor** cortex, which enables him to move his fingers, **(3) sensory** cortex, which enables him to see and feel the strings and hear the music, and **(4) association** areas, which are involved in reading music and playing the guitar. Information received on one side of the brain crosses to the other side via the **(5) corpus callosum,** which results in the integrated activity of both sides of the brain. At the same time, Matthews' body maintains its basic functions. Heartbeat, breathing, and other vital systems are controlled by the **(6) medulla,** and, in order to maintain his attention on the guitar, arousal is controlled by the **(7) reticular formation.** Behind Matthews' talent and skills are two more important brain structures: the **(8) hippocampus,** which is involved in his memory of how to play the guitar and of musical scales and time signatures, and the **(9) cerebellum,** which helps coordinate movements involved in playing the guitar.

Chapter 3
Nature, Nurture, and Human Diversity

Review 3.1: Genetics

Jennifer and Brad have decided to have a child. At conception, Jennifer's **(1) egg** and Brad's **(2) sperm** each contribute 23 threadlike structures, or **(3) chromosomes.** These structures are contained in the

(4) nucleus of each of the trillions of cells in Baby JB's body, and they are made of a coiled chain of the molecule **(5) DNA,** which is divided into segments called **(6) genes,** which, when expressed, form templates for the production of **(7) protein** molecules, thus determining JB's individual physical **(8) (biological)** development and forming the complete instructions, or **(9) genome,** for uniquely making JB. Groups of the self-replicating biochemical units acting together, called **(10) gene complexes,** influence most human traits, including simple **(11) physical** traits, such as height and weight, and more complex **(12) psychological** traits, such as aggression and musical ability. Despite her uniqueness, JB is **(13) 96** percent genetically the same as Washoe the chimp (see Chapter 10).

Review 3.2: Nature and Nurture

JB's genetic inheritance, her nature, does not work in a vacuum. At every level and in every way, nature interacts with **(1) nurture,** the environment to which JB is exposed. Like the rest of our species, JB has an enormous **(2) adaptive** capacity. As she grows up, she may prefer eating Boston baked beans or refried beans, depending on the tastes she learns from her surrounding **(3) culture.** The interaction of heredity and environment began when JB was **(4) conceived,** and she was affected by the **(5) prenatal** environment of Jen's womb, including the **(6) nutrition** she received from what Jen ate and any toxic agents Jen was exposed to. If JB had a twin (BJ), the similarity of their environmental influences prenatally would depend on whether the twins shared the same **(7) placenta.** After birth, JB is affected by several environments: Experience helps develop her brain's **(8) synaptic connections;** her family environment has a strong influence on her **(9) political** attitudes, **(10) religious** beliefs, and personal manners; peer influence occurs through a **(11) selection** effect, as JB finds friends with similar attitudes and interests; and finally, JB follows the rules of accepted and expected behavior, or **(12) norms,** of her culture.

Review 3.3: Gender Differences

Now suppose that JB has a brother Bruno, who is a few years younger. Assume that JB and Bruno are an average female and male. Compared to Bruno, JB has a body with more **(1) fat** and less **(2) muscle,** begins puberty about **(3) two** years earlier, and is expected to outlive him by about **(4) five** years. Psychologically, JB and Bruno are different in several ways: JB is more vulnerable to **(5) depression, (6) anxiety,** and **(7) eating** disorders. Bruno is more likely to commit **(8) suicide,** to suffer **(9) alcoholism,** and to be **(10) hyperactive** as a child. In terms of social power, JB is perceived as having more traditionally **(11) feminine** traits, such as being more deferential, nurturing, and affiliative. Bruno is perceived as having more traditionally **(12) masculine** traits, such as being more dominant, directive, and autocratic, and talking more assertively. In terms of social connectedness, JB is more **(13) interdependent**—and likely to tend and **(14) befriend.** Bruno tends to emphasize **(15) self-reliance** and freedom.

Chapter 4
Developing Through the Life Span

Review 4.1: Physical Development

Jorge and Sonya Nuñez have a son named Felipe. Felipe started out as a fertilized egg, or **(1) zygote,** whose cells quickly began to **(2) divide.** Two weeks into **(3) prenatal** development, his organs began to form and function, and he was referred to as an **(4) embryo.** As Felipe became more human in appearance, about 9 weeks after conception, he was called a **(5) fetus.** Throughout this process, Felipe's genes interacted with the **(6) environment,** and Felipe was protected by the **(7) placenta,** which prevented many harmful substances from reaching him, and because Sonya didn't drink alcohol, Felipe was NOT exposed to this harmful **(8) teratogen** and will not be at risk of developing **(9) fetal alcohol syndrome.** As a newborn, Felipe came equipped with a variety of **(10) reflexes** suited to survival, including the tendency to turn toward Sonya when she touched him on the cheek, called the **(11) rooting reflex.** Felipe is now an infant, and his biological and psychological development continues, depending to a large extent on the rapid development of his brain's **(12) frontal** lobes, with the last areas of the brain to develop being those linked with thinking, memory, and language—the **(13) association** areas of the cortex. As his genes continue to direct his biological growth through the process called **(14) maturation,** Felipe begins to sit, crawl, stand, walk, and then run. This **(15) sequence** of motor development is universal; the **(16) timing** is not.

Felipe is now a teenager, an adolescent who has just attained sexual maturity, or **(17) puberty.** His younger sister, Elena, has reached the same stage, but she is only **(18) 11** years old. During the growth spurt that follows, their reproductive organs—his testes and her ovaries, or **(19) primary sexual characteristics**—develop dramatically, while Elena's breasts and hips and Felipe's voice and body hair, or **(20) secondary sexual characteristics,** also begin to develop. When Jorge and Sonya criticize their children's clothing, hairstyle, or the friends they bring home, Felipe storms outside, slamming the door behind him, and Elena retreats to her room, iPod in hand. Their behavior can be blamed in part on the early development of the brain's emotional **(21) limbic system.** Fortunately, this is followed by selective **(22) pruning** of unused neurons and connections and the growth of fatty **(23) myelin** tissue in the frontal lobes, which leads to improved judgment and impulse control. Adulthood brings benefits and challenges: Both Felipe and Elena can maintain physical vigor if they have good **(24) health** habits. For Elena, biological aging is signaled by the end of menstruation, or **(25) menopause,** which is accompanied by a reduction in the hormone **(26) estrogen.** For Felipe, there is no comparable loss of **(27) fertility,** but there is a gradual decline in sperm count and lower levels of the hormone **(28) testosterone.** In old age, their **(29) immune** systems weaken, and they are **(30) more** susceptible to life-threatening illnesses and **(31) less** susceptible to short-term illnesses.

Review 4.2: Cognitive Development

The Nuñez family lives in the city. Every year, beginning when the children are very young, they vacation on a farm. In the city, the children see many dogs and develop a concept, or **(1) schema,** for four-legged animals. On the farm, they see pigs and goats and try to **(2) assimilate** these animals into their dog concept, but Sonya corrects them and identifies the animals as separate concepts, so the children have to **(3) accommodate** their schemas to their new experiences. Also according to Jean **(4) Piaget,** the mind develops through a series of **(5) stages** as we continually modify our thinking to fit the particulars of new experiences. At age 1, Elena puts all objects—rattles, keys, anything within reach—into her mouth. She's in the **(6) sensorimotor** stage. If the rattle is hidden, Elena knows it's still there somewhere and will search for it. She has developed **(7) object permanence.** At age 3, Felipe has an imaginary friend and can describe events with words, and so is in the **(8) preoperational** stage. He doesn't understand that water in an inverted beaker could be the same amount as water in a rightside-up beaker—the concept of **(9) conservation**—and when he covers his eyes, he thinks no one can see him, which means he is **(10) egocentric.** When Elena is 6 and Felipe is 8, they can understand that the two beakers contain the same amount, and so they are in the **(11) concrete** operational stage. According to Lawrence **(12) Kohlberg,** Felipe and Elena have probably developed a **(13) preconventional** morality based on a desire to avoid punishment or gain rewards.

With adolescence comes newfound reasoning abilities and a strong moral sense: Now in the **(14) formal operational** stage, Felipe and Elena think about such abstract concepts as war, justice, and democracy, and their morality has evolved to a more **(15) conventional** level, based on upholding laws and obeying rules. Jorge and Sonya, who are now in their 50s, join their children, who are in their 20s, in a memory test. Research indicates that Felipe and Elena will be better at **(16) recalling** information, while Jorge and Sonya will excel at **(17) recognizing** information. Also, Mom and Pop's ability to solve Sudoku puzzles (to reason speedily), reflected in their **(18) fluid** intelligence, will decline, while their ability to win at Scrabble (to have a large vocabulary), reflected in their **(19) crystallized** intelligence, will increase. At first, researchers thought intelligence generally declined with age. This was because they compared the test scores of people of different ages, using the **(20) cross-sectional** method, while newer research, using the **(21) longitudinal** method, showed that intelligence remained stable until late in life.

Review 4.3: Social Development

Many years later, Elena's daughter Leah asks her 90-year-old grandmother Sonya about her early life. Sonya tells Leah, "I had a wonderful childhood, with loving parents who made me feel safe and secure." Developmental theorist Erik **(1) Erikson** might say that this secure **(2) attachment** allowed Sonya to develop a sense of **(3) basic trust.** As a toddler, Sonya was encouraged to try new things and was applauded for her efforts. She developed a sense of independence or **(4) autonomy,** rather than the shame and **(5) doubt** that could have occurred during this stage. All of this was possible because her parents were demanding but warm and responsive, or **(6) authoritative**—not lenient, as **(7) permissive** parents may be, or extremely strict and demanding as **(8) authoritarian** parents are. This parenting style contributed to Sonya's high **(9) self-esteem** and her **(10) social** competence. As a child in school, when Sonya began learning how to read and write, she developed a sense of **(11) competence** rather than inferiority and a clear sense of her own identity and personal worth, or a **(12) self-concept.**

As a teenager, Sonya was aggressive and opinionated with her friends but shy and agreeable with her parents until she finally merged these different selves into a consistent **(13) identity.** During high school, Sonya moved from small groups of girlfriends to mixed groups of boys and girls to dating one boy. Along the way, she learned about relationships and developed a capacity for **(14) intimacy,** thus avoiding a sense of social **(15) isolation.** Then, following the culturally preferred timing of social events, or the **(16) social clock,** she married her childhood sweetheart, Jorge, after college. They both had fulfilling careers while raising a loving, caring family. Sonya says, "These contributions to the world and to future generations have given Jorge and me a strong sense of **(17) generativity,** unlike mean old Mr. Ramirez across the street, whose life has been purposeless." Erikson would say Ramirez is **(18) stagnant.** Sonya continued, "As your grandfather and I look back on our lives, we are content. Our lives have been meaningful and worthwhile; we have a sense of **(19) integrity** rather than the despair felt by Mr. Ramirez."

Chapter 5
Sensation

Review 5.1: Vision
Jamail is a software engineer who is animating a new soccer computer game. The visible light from the computer screen, which is only a small portion of the **(1) electromagnetic** spectrum of energy, has two physical characteristics: the distance from one wave peak to the next is its **(2) wavelength,** which determines the **(3) hue**—for example, the blue shorts and green background Jamail has chosen for his animation—and the height, or **(4) amplitude,** from peak to trough of the wave, which determines the amount of energy in a light wave, or its **(5) intensity,** which we perceive as brightness. For Jamail's eyes to see, they must transform particles of light energy into colorful objects in this sequence: Light enters Jamail's eyes through the protective **(6) cornea** and then passes through a small opening, the **(7) pupil,** which is regulated by a colored muscle, the **(8) iris.** Next, light passes through the **(9) lens,** which, by a process called **(10) accommodation,** focuses the light on the eye's **(11) retina.** When the image from the computer screen reaches Jamail's retina, it stimulates two receptor cells: the **(12) rods,** in the periphery, for black-and-white vision, and the **(13) cones,** in the fovea, for color vision, which stimulate the **(14) bipolar** cells, which then activate the **(15) ganglion** cells, whose axons form the **(16) optic** nerve that carries information to Jamail's **(17) brain.**

Review 5.2: Hearing
As Jamail programs the new soccer computer game, he is careful to adjust the sound track in order to regulate the sound waves' two physical characteristics: the waves' length, which determines their **(1) frequency,** which we perceive as **(2) pitch,** and the strength, or **(3) amplitude** of the waves, which we perceive as **(4) loudness.** Jamail is able to perceive these psychological properties of sound, because the sound waves enter his outer ear and are channeled through the **(5) auditory** canal to the membrane that vibrates in response to the pressure, which is called the **(6) eardrum.** The vibrations are then transmitted to three tiny bones: the **(7) hammer, (8) anvil,** and **(9) stirrup,** which cause the **(10) oval window** of the snail-shaped tube called the **(11) cochlea** to vibrate. In this tube, the vibrations from Jamail's characters' screams, grunts, and groans cause fluid to move, creating

ripples in the **(12) basilar membrane**, which is lined with **(13) hair cells** that bend, triggering impulses in **(14) nerve** fibers that form the **(15) auditory** nerve, which sends the information to the auditory **(16) cortex** in the brain's **(17) temporal** lobe.

Review 5.3: Pain

Jamail has spent so many hours on the computer, hand wrapped around the mouse, that his middle fingers feel numb and pain is shooting up his arm. According to the **(1) gate-control** theory, Jamail's spinal cord contains two types of fibers: small fibers, which **(2) open** the gate to the brain, so that Jamail **(3) does** feel pain, and large fibers, which **(4) close** the gate to the brain, so that Jamail **(5) does not** feel pain. Because Jamail has an approaching deadline, he plods on. He belongs to a **(6) culture** that encourages stoicism in the face of pain. Also, he is **(7) distracted** from the pain by thoughts of the deadline as well as by the cool snow scenes in the cyber environment in which he is operating to create his game, which is similar to **(8) virtual-reality** pain control.

Review 5.4: Hearing, Smell, Taste, and Interaction

It's time for Jamail to take a break. He closes his eyes to relax, but the phone, which is to the left of him, rings. With his eyes still closed, he is able to pick up the phone. He does this because the **(1) just noticeable difference** of the sound reaching his two ears tells his sense of **(2) kinesthesis** where to move his hand. Jamail's ability illustrates the concept that one sense may influence another, which is called **(3) sensory interaction.** This principle works for all of his senses. For example, Jamail finishes talking to his friend and goes to the kitchen for a snack, where the smell of freshly baked bread activates the receptors in the **(4) olfactory** membrane, which transmits electric signals to higher regions of the brain by way of converged **(5) axons.** Because the receptors for smell are located near the brain's ancient **(6) limbic** centers, the smell of the bread evokes **(7) memories** of his childhood, when his mother spent Saturdays baking for the family. Jamail takes a piece of bread. Adding to the smell and texture of the bread, his taste **(8) buds** give him the flavor of banana bread, and this information is sent to the brain's **(9) temporal** lobe, which is near where olfactory information is received.

Chapter 6
Perception

Review 6.1: Three-Dimensional Perception

Bethany is a member of Gamma University's bowling team, and she's been selected to play against nearby Alpha University. Besides physical dexterity, she depends on **(1) depth** perception to estimate the distance and angle of the ball from the pins she is trying to knock down. Visual cues are the source of this perception. Using both eyes, the **(2) binocular** cues help Bethany bowl a great game. The brain compares the difference, or **(3) retinal disparity,** of the images from her right and left eyes, telling her that the 1 pin is closer than the 5 pin behind it. The inward turning of the eye, required for focusing, which is called **(4) convergence,** also tells her that the 1 pin is closer. Each eye also provides **(5) monocular** cues that contribute to her accurate bowling. For example, she knows that the 8 pin is farther away from her than the 5 pin because of the difference in the **(6) relative size** of the images that the bowling pins cast on her retina and the fact that the 5 pin appears **(7) lighter** than the 8 pin, while the 8 pin is **(8) higher** in her field of vision. Also the 5 pin partially blocks her view of the 8 pin, a cue called **(9) interposition.**

Review 6.2: Perceptual Interpretation

Kurt is now a college junior with perfect vision. However, he was born with an opaque lens, or **(1) cataracts,** in each eye, which were surgically corrected when he was an infant. If Kurt's vision had not been restored until he was an adult, philosopher Immanuel **(2) Kant** would have predicted that Kurt would have difficulty visually identifying objects learned from touch, while philosopher John **(3) Locke,** who believed that knowledge comes from **(4) learned** ways of organizing sensory information, would have disagreed. Today, Kurt is a criminal science major because his goal is to work in law enforcement. His friends tease him that he has a mental predisposition, or **(5) mental set** to "see" crime and violence everywhere he looks. A psychologist might say that his education and interests have shaped his perceptual concepts, or **(6) schemas.** For example, when shown this reversible **(7) figure-ground** drawing at left, which can be seen as either people hurrying or arrowheads, Kurt readily perceives "violent men charging" as the **(8) figure** and the white arrowheads as the **(9) ground.**

Chapter 7
States of Consciousness

Review 7.1: Biological Rhythms and Sleep

This doctor worked the night shift for 6 months and has now switched to days. Clearly, he has not yet succeeded in resetting his 24-hour **(1) biological clock.** He would be well advised to spend some time outdoors during the day because bright light activates **(2) proteins** in his eyes' **(3) retinas,** which trigger signals to the brain's **(4) suprachiasmatic** nucleus, causing the **(5) pineal** gland to decrease production of the sleep-inducing hormone **(6) melatonin.** Being sleep deprived, this doctor may experience a depressed **(7) immune** system, impaired **(8) performance,** and impaired concentration—not what you want in someone who is treating an illness or injury. So, the doctor finally gets some sleep, passing through the five sleep stages, preceded by the relaxed, awake state characterized by regular **(9) alpha** waves. In Stage 1, he may feel he is falling, a **(10) hypnagogic** sensation, and have false sensory experiences, or **(11) hallucinations.** In Stage 2, his brain generates bursts of rapid activity, or sleep **(12) spindles.** In Stages 3 and 4, **(13) deep** sleep, he experiences large, slow **(14) delta** waves. When waves become rapid and saw-toothed and eyes dart about, he has entered **(15) REM** sleep, where he **(16) dreams** of making a major medical breakthrough.

Review 7.2: Drug Abuse

Jack believes that three main influences may contribute to his neighbor Brian's heavy drinking: Brian's parents have a history of alcoholism, so he may have a **(1) genetic** predisposition. Brian's life has been significantly disrupted by the drinking, which suggests an underlying **(2) addiction.** Brian spends a lot of time with friends at the local bar, which suggests that **(3) social** influence is also significant. Since Jack moved in 5 years ago, Brian's drinking has increased, most likely because a few beers have less effect on Brian (he's developed a **(4) tolerance** for alcohol), and his brain is experiencing **(5) neuroadaptation** as it attempts to counteract the effects of the alcohol. In addition, to cope with stress, Brian has at least a few beers every day, indicating that he has developed **(6) psychological** dependence, while his daily cravings for alcohol suggest that he may also have developed a **(7) physical** dependence. Jack is particularly worried about the effects on Brian's mind and body: Alcohol is a kind of psychoactive drug called a **(8) depressant,** because it physically slows down activity in the **(9) central** nervous system, causes Brian's brain to **(10) shrink,** and boosts activity in the brain's **(11) dopamine** reward system. Psychologically, alcohol lower **(12) inhibitions,** impairs judgment and **(13) memory,** and causes Brian to lose **(14) self-restraint.**

Chapter 8
Learning

Review 8.1: Classical Conditioning

Antonia lives in Alaska. She loves walking through falling snow and feeling the wet snowflakes on her face. Whenever a snowflake—the **(1) unconditioned stimulus**—falls into her eye, it triggers an eyeblink, which is the **(2) unconditioned response.** Coincidentally, each time a snowflake falls into her eye, the school bell rings, which is a **(3) conditioned stimulus.** And, after several pairings with the snowflake in the eye, the bell also begins to trigger an eyeblink, and so it is now the **(4) conditioned response.** This is the **(5) acquisition** stage of classical conditioning. While in school, the bell rings between class periods, but, of course, there are no snowflakes, which results in **(6) extinction** of

Antonia's eyeblink response. At recess, another snowflake falls into her eye just as the warning bell rings to go back inside. When the final bell rings a few minutes later, Antonia finds herself blinking, which shows that she has experienced **(7) spontaneous recovery** of her eyeblink response to the bell. If a clock chime similar to the original school bell were to be presented, responding with the eyeblink would represent **(8) generalization.** Not responding to the similar stimulus would represent **(9) discrimination.**

Review 8.2: Operant Conditioning

Leon is trying to teach his cat to jump through a hoop. A small treat, a **(1) primary** reinforcer, or rubbing the cat's ears, a **(2) conditioned** reinforcer, can be used to train or **(3) shape** this jumping behavior. In teaching the cat to jump through the hoop, Leon tries two different **(4) variable reinforcement** schedules. First he tries rewarding the cat after different amounts of time which is a **(5) variable-interval** schedule. Next, he tries rewarding the cat after different numbers of correct responses (jumping through the hoop), a **(6) variable-ratio** schedule. The steadiest rate of responding occurs with a **(7) variable-ratio** schedule. Leon chose jumping through a hoop because of the cat's **(8) biological predisposition** to jump high and land on its feet.

Review 8.3: Learning by Observation

According to pioneering researcher Albert **(1) Bandura,** we learn not only by association but also by **(2) modeling (imitating)** the behavior of people who are successful, admirable, and **(3) similar** to us. For example, during holiday breaks, Lionel watcher *Monday Night Raw,* a World Wrestling Entertainment extravaganza, which **(4) increases** his aggressive tendencies. His brother Michael won't watch the wrestling, because he feels the pain of a choke hold, for example, as reflected in his brain's **(5) mirror neurons.** Instead, Michael spends time with Grandma, who cooks for the poor during the holiday season, helping Michael to learn **(6) prosocial** behavior.

CHAPTER 9
Memory

Review 9.1: Information Processing

Elizabeth is studying for a psychology exam on learning. First, information must be detected in her **(1) sensory** memory, which consists of the words in her text (visual sensory memory, called **(2) iconic** memory) and her instructor's lectures (auditory sensory memory, called **(3) echoic** memory). If Liz pays attention to the information, she will encode it, so that the **(4) episodic** buffer can begin processing the information in **(5) working** memory, which is managed by a **(6) central executive** that integrates incoming information with stored memories. During this stage, information is processed by two subsystems: auditory **(7) rehearsal,** where Liz repeats US, UR, and so on until the concepts stay with her, and the **(8) visual-spatial** sketchpad, which allows Liz to visualize the Chapter 8 text pages where classical conditioning is discussed.

In order to encode the information, Liz uses a variety of techniques: processing the **(9) meaning** of UR, by associating the term *unconditioned responses* with the word *involuntary,* picturing a dog drooling at the sight of food, or using **(10) visual imagery,** and **(11) organizing** the information by noting the sequence of events in classical conditioning, either by **(12) chunking,** or grouping the concepts, by stages or by creating a flow chart that places the events in a **(13) hierarchy.** Assuming that Liz's efforts have enabled her to store the information, she must now get the information out of storage. She must **(14) retrieve** it from the relatively limitless, permanent storehouse of information called **(15) long-term** memory, which includes conscious recall. Her declarative or **(16) explicit memory** consists of **(17) facts,** such as the definitions of US, CS, UR, and CR, and **(18) personally experienced** events, such as having actually seen a dog drooling over food. Her memory also includes unconscious recollection. Her procedural or **(19) implicit memory** consists of **(20) motor** and cognitive skills, such as knowing how to take notes, and things she's learned by way of **(21) classical** and **(22) operant** conditioning effects, such as associating a fresh cup of coffee and her desk with study time.

Review 9.2: Forgetting

As a senior member of her high school swim team, Melissa is rewarded with a large locker. She learns the new combination, but then she can't remember the code for the old padlock on her bike; this is an example of **(1) retroactive interference.** After practice, while Melissa is struggling with the padlock, two new team members pass by. She says, "Hi, Rebecca," but realizes she's now the victim of **(2) proactive interference,** because Rebecca is the name of a teammate who graduated last year. Both of these reasons for forgetting are forms of **(3) retrieval** failure, because in both cases, the information was in long-term memory. An alternative explanation for Melissa's memory problems is that she never actually **(4) encoded** the new information into long-term memory. During practice, the coach referred to a pep talk, which she said Melissa had given before last year's championship meet. But, in fact, Rebecca had given the pep talk. Melissa's coach is suffering from **(5) source** amnesia, possibly because Melissa had provided **(6) misleading** information by referring to her ability to urge her teammates on. Melissa's Aunt Kate is so fearful of water that she can't even attend her niece's swim meets, but she doesn't know why she is fearful. Sigmund **(7) Freud** might have suggested that Kate has **(8) repressed** a traumatic childhood incident, which left her with this disruptive fear. Contemporary researchers **(9) disagree** with the psychoanalytic view of forgetting.

CHAPTER 10
Thinking and Language

Review 10.1: Problem Solving

Pierre is applying to the Delicioso Culinary Institute. To qualify, he must prepare a special recipe of his own design, so he practices at home. At first, he tries mixing different ingredients to create a unique pasta sauce. This hit-and-miss method is referred to as **(1) trial** and **(2) error.** After tossing out several "yucky" recipes, he learns more about which herbs mix well together and in what order, and so he writes out a recipe, a step-by-step procedure, or **(3) algorithm,** for an unbelievaby "delicioso" pasta sauce. Pierre takes the test, is accepted by the Institute, and, several years later, is hired as "Chef to the Stars." Guided by his experience, Pierre uses a simple thinking strategy, or **(4) heuristic,** to create many more awesome recipes, and occasionally, he creates a recipe that comes to him in a flash of inspiration, or **(5) insight.** While Pierre is successfully building a career as a world-renowned chef, his friend André (who also wants to be a chef) has not done well. André's attempts to create original recipes have been hindered by his inability to look at a problem from a fresh perspective. This **(6) fixation** may be in the form of a **(7) mental set,** or a tendency to approach a problem with what has worked before—for example, always broiling pork chops when pan-frying might work well—**(8) functional fixedness,** or a tendency to think of things in terms of their usual functions—for example, thinking basil can be used only for flavoring spaghetti sauce when it's also "delicioso" in meat loaf. André blames his failure on his own misuse of problem-solving techniques. In creating recipes, he was affected by the **(9) availability heuristic,** because he only tried the combinations that came readily to mind rather than thinking outside the box about other possibilities. He was also overly affected by the **(10) representative heuristic** when he chose only the ingredients that matched his prototype for pasta sauces.

Review 10.2: Language Development

Erika and Jason have twins: Spencer was born with normal hearing, and Sheila was born deaf. Erika and Jason have therefore learned American Sign Language. The children **(1) did** pass through the same sequence of stages of language development, which began at 2 or 3 months of age, with **(2) babbling,** or uttering sounds that can be found in all languages. By their second birthday, both children had entered into the **(3) two-word** stage, in which Spencer's words and Sheila's hand signs are mostly **(4) nouns** and **(5) verbs,** which is referred to as **(6) telegraphic speech.** In Spencer's spoken words, the basic sounds, such as *ba, da,* and *ma,* are called **(7) phonemes,** and those sounds form the smallest unit of meaningful language, such as *dad,* which is a **(8) morpheme.** Sounds and words derive meaning based on the set of language rules we call **(9) semantics.** The rules for ordering words are referred to as the **(10) syntax** of the language's grammar. Psychologists agree that Spencer and Sheila's rapid acquisition of productive language depended on their exposure to language during a **(11) critical** period of development. Psychologists disagree on how language develops. Behaviorists such as B. F. **(12) Skinner** contend that Sheila and Spencer learned by **(13) associating** objects with words, **(14) imitating** other people's speech or hand signals, and being **(15) reinforced** with a smile for saying or signing correctly. Linguist Noam **(16) Chomsky** agrees that children learn from their environment, but he feels that they acquire untaught words and grammar too quickly to be explained solely by **(17) learning** principles. Instead, he contends that all languages have the same basic building blocks and that therefore there is a **(18) universal grammar,** and that all children—hearing or deaf— are born with a **(19) language acquisition** device. In support of this linguist's theory, cognitive neuroscientists have found that we learn new languages easily as a **(20) young** person and that language learning grows **(21) harder** with age.

CHAPTER 11
Intelligence

Review 11.1: What Is Intelligence?

Retief and Ron are university friends and are discussing their future plans. Ron says, "I have an IQ of 120." Retief points out that Ron is **(1) reifying** the concept of intelligence and should instead say, "My score on an intelligence test was 120." Retief, who's been studying intelligence in his psychology textbook, continues by noting that he agrees with historical researcher Charles **(2) Spearman,** who suggested that there is a **(3) general intelligence,** or *g,* factor that underlies various clusters of abilities. Knowing that Ron is a World Checkers Champion, Retief isn't sure that Ron's verbal intelligence would show up in a cluster with his truly amazing spatial abilities if **(4) factor analysis** were used on the results of his intelligence test. Retief, on the other hand, who is a wonderful piano keyboarder, agrees with psychologist Robert **(5) Sternberg,** who has suggested that there are three intelligences and that Retief's ability to produce unique sound combinations reflects his **(6) creative** intelligence, while his friend Ron's spatial abilities would be considered **(7) analytical** intelligence. Their friend Sho, who also achieves a high IQ score, has decided to become a psychotherapist. Sho has very high **(8) emotional** intelligence, which enables him to perceive, **(9) understand, (10) manage,** and use emotions.

Review 11.2: History of Intelligence Testing

In 1904, the French minister of public education wanted to find an objective way of identifying children with special needs. He asked Alfred **(1) Binet** to study the problem. Assuming that all children follow **(2) the same** course of intellectual development, he and Théodore **(3) Simon** devised the first intelligence test to assess learning potential. They measured the child's **(4) mental** age, defined as the **(5) chronological** age typical of a given level of performance. Years later, Lewis **(6) Terman** found that this test did not work well with California students and so revised it to create the **(7) Stanford-Binet** test, which formed the basis for William **(8) Stern's** intelligence quotient (IQ) formula: **(9) mental** age divided by **(10) chronological** age, and multiply the result by 100. Using this formula, the average score is **(11) 100.** Because the original IQ formula worked fairly well for **(12) children** but not for **(13) adults,** today's intelligence tests instead produce a mental ability score based on the test-taker's performance relative to the average performance of others the same **(14) age.**

Review 11.3: Assessing Intelligence

Eighteeen-year-old Sooji is designing an intelligence test that will predict how well her peers will fare as they go on to higher education by assessing their **(1) aptitude** for advanced learning. After creating the questions, Sooji must make sure the test meets the criteria of a good psychological test.

First, she administers the test to a **(2) representative** sample of students, creating a pretested group against which test-takers' scores can be compared in order to **(3) standardize** the test. Next, she must be sure that the test yields consistent results, perhaps by comparing answers to odd and even questions—that it is **(4) reliable.** Finally, she must be sure the test measures and predicts what it is supposed to—that it is **(5) valid.** If the test measures students' academic potential, then it has **(6) content** validity, because it is indeed measuring the behavior of interest. And if the test scores later correlate with the behavior they were attempting to predict, known as the **(7) criterion,** then the test has **(8) predictive** validity. If Sooji's test meets all the criteria of a good psychological test, as David **(9) Wechsler's** intelligence scale does, the scores of any group of people who take it should form a bell-shaped pattern called a **(10) normal** curve, with an average score of **(11) 100.** To keep that average score, Sooji must periodically **(12) re-standardize** the test. And, if Sooji had first developed and administered her test 30 years ago, then compared the scores with the scores of today's students, she'd find that they had increased, which is called the **(13) Flynn** effect.

CHAPTER 12
Motivation and Work

Review 12.1: Hunger and Eating Behavior

Sitting in her afternoon psychology class, Erica regrets skipping breakfast and lunch. As a biology major, she knows that her hunger pangs, caused by stomach **(1) contractions,** signal increased secretion of two chemical messengers, or **(2) hormones: (3) insulin** from the pancreas and **(4) ghrelin** from her empty stomach. Erica is having trouble keeping her eyes open during class (even though Professor Straub is a stimulating lecturer), because the increased secretion from her pancreas reduces the level of her body's energy fuel, **(5) glucose,** in the bloodstream. However, Erica's brain isn't sleeping through class. In fact, her brain's **(6) lateral hypothalamus** has been secreting the hunger-triggering hormone **(7) orexin,** and so a very hungry Erica heads home for a large bowl of pasta. She finally feels full, a sensation triggered by activity in the brain's **(8) ventromedial hypothalamus.** After eating, Erica weighs herself: She's 5'6" tall and weighs about 118 pounds, well below the 130-pound normal weight for her height, but she feels fat and, vowing to lose some weight, she takes a laxative, a clear symptom of an **(9) eating disorder.** Erica's obsession with her weight has a few possible explanations: One might be a **(10) negative** self-evaluation. Or she may have internalized and become obsessed with her Western **(11) culture's** "thin ideal." Another possibility is that she may be **(12) genetically** susceptible to eating disorders.

Review 12.2: Sexual Orientation

Max's parents are finding it difficult to accept that he is gay. Max explains that he **(1) did not** choose his sexual orientation and that he **(2) cannot** change. His parents want to understand why Max feels as he does, so Max begins by discounting all the myths he's sure they've heard. Max tells them that he does not fear the other sex, he was not smothered by **(3) motherly** love or neglected by his **(4) father,** he was not **(5) molested** as a child, and that he was not segregated by gender during **(6) puberty,** and he does not fear or hate **(7) women.** Max notes that the most recent research evidence indicates a **(8) biological** basis for one's sexual orientation. For example, researchers have found that a cell cluster in the **(9) hypothalamus** and a section of the **(10) anterior commissure** are larger in homosexual men, and that between the middle of the **(11) second and fifth** months after conception, exposure to **(12) hormone** levels typically experienced by a **(13) female** fetus may predispose homosexuality in males. Max continues to explain that there is also evidence of a **(14) genetic** link: (1) homosexuality tends to run in families, especially on the **(15) mother's** side; (2) twin studies show that **(16) identical** twins are more likely than **(17) fraternal** twins to share a sexual orientation, and (3) research with fruit flies has shown that **(18) genetic manipulation** can determine sexual orientation.

Review 12.3: Motivation and Work

Tonya wants to apply her knowledge of psychology in a corporate setting, so she is taking courses in **(1) industrial-organizational** psychology. She already knows that she doesn't want to work in human factors psychology, but now she must decide whether she wants to help match workers to skills as a **(2) personnel** psychologist, or she may want to help motivate workers and improve an organization's infrastructure, as an **(3) organizational** psychologist. Tonya must also consider which type of work makes her feel happiest, most focused, and most involved, in other words, experience **(4) flow.** For example, she may feel happiest analyzing a job, scripting questions, and training interviewers to avoid the interviewer **(5) illusion** and perform a **(6) structured** interview that will pinpoint potential employees' strengths. Or she may prefer working directly with employees, focusing on their **(7) achievement motivation** by encouraging them to attain a high standard, and attempting to increase employee **(8) engagement** by finding ways for them to feel involved and satisfied with their work. Part of Tonya's work in motivating employees would involve teaching managers effective management techniques. She would encourage managers to choose an appropriate **(9) leadership** style, harness **(10) job-relevant** strengths, and set specific, challenging **(11) goals.** In selecting a leadership style, managers must choose between goal-oriented **(12) task** leadership or group-oriented **(13) social** leadership, and work toward managing with self-confident charisma. They also know that the most successful leaders tend to have a **(14) vision** of a goal, an ability to **(15) communicate** it clearly, and enough optimism and faith in the group to **(16) inspire** others.

CHAPTER 13
Emotion

Review 13.1: Theories of Emotion

Walking home from school after the basketball game, Jesse takes a shortcut through an area with no street lights. He sees a shadow of a person with something glistening in his hand, which causes him to experience the three parts of a distinct emotion. Thinking the shiny object is a knife, Jesse's heart begins to pound, which is part of his **(1) physiological** arousal. Jesse attempts to flee, which is his **(2) expressive** behavior. He is afraid of being stabbed, which is his **(3) conscious** experience of the situation. Different theories have been proposed to explain Jesse's emotional experience. Perception of man with knife (stimulus) leads to Theory 1: a pounding heart (**(4) physiological** arousal) leads to fear, which is the experienced **(5) emotion.** This is the **(6) James-Lange** theory of emotion. Theory 2: a pounding heart (**(7) physiological arousal)** and simultaneous **(8) subjective** experience of the fear emotion. This is the **(9) Cannon-Bard** theory of emotion. Theory 3: a pounding heart (**(10) physiological arousal)** and simultaneous "Man with knife scares me." (**(11) cognitive label)** leads to the experience of fear. This is the **(12) two-factor** theory of emotion.

Review 13.2: Embodied Emotion

On her way to class this morning, Rena swerved her car to the right to avoid being hit by a motorist veering into her lane. Her physiological arousal was triggered by the **(1) sympathetic** division of her **(2) autonomic** nervous system, which directed her **(3) adrenal** glands to release the stress hormones **(4) epinephrine** and **(5) norepinephrine,** which increased her **(6) heart** rate, blood **(7) pressure,** and blood **(8) sugar (glucose)** levels. Rena responded quickly because the fear message was routed directly (via the **(9) thalamus**) to her **(10) amygdala,** the brain's emotional center. By the time Rena reached the classroom, the **(11) parasympathetic** division had calmed her body. If she could have had a PET scan during class when she learned that she earned a perfect score on a term paper, she would have seen that her brain's **(12) left frontal** lobe showed increased activity, perhaps because of the rich supply of **(13) dopamine** receptors in that area. After class, Rena changed in the locker room and went for her afternoon run. Later, in an aroused state from the exercise and the good news about her term paper, Rena smiled at a frolicking child. This response, called the **(14) spillover** effect, results from cognitive analysis as the sensory input passes through her brain's **(15) prefrontal cortex.**

Review 13.3: Happiness

Alycia is in a good mood because she just learned that a good friend is coming to visit tomorrow. On her way home, she sees an infant drop her pacifier. Alycia picks it up cheerfully for the young mother, a reflection of the **(1) feel-good, do-good** phenomenon. As she is walking home, Alycia thinks: "I'm pretty lucky—I'm young and healthy, and I have lots of close friends. And, I have a $1000 scholarship to the university of my choice." Researchers in the new field of **(2) positive** psychology would say that her life satisfaction, or **(3) subjective** well-being, is high. A few days later, Alycia learns that her friend Lois has received a scholarship that will pay all her higher education tuition. Comparing her meager scholarship to Lois' full scholarship reduces Alycia's satisfaction, producing in her a sense of **(4) relative** deprivation. Being a generally positive person, however, with a more active **(5) left frontal** lobe in her brain and high **(6) self-esteem,** Alycia judges her current financial status against her prior financial problems and feels content, which psychologists refer to as the **(7) adaptation-level** phenomenon.

Chapter 14
Stress and Health

Review 14.1: Stress and the Body's Responses

Instead of studying, Jennifer went out with her friends last night, so she's poorly prepared for today's biology exam. Her level of stress is high because she is thinking about, or **(1) appraising,** this particular **(2) stressor,** or test, as beyond her coping abilities. Jennifer's response was first described by Walter **(3) Cannon** and later refined by physiologists who identified a **(4) two-track (dual-track)** system, in which the **(5) sympathetic** nervous system directs the **(6) adrenal** glands to release the stress hormones **(7) epinephrine** and **(8) norepinephrine.** These hormones are responsible for Jennifer's **(9) immediate** response to stress. At the same time, the brain's **(10) cerebral cortex,** by way of the **(11) hypothalamus** and the pituitary gland, directs the **(12) adrenal** glands to release the **(13) glucocorticoid** stress hormones, such as **(14) cortisol.** These hormones are responsible for Jennifer's **(15) sustained** response to stress. When stressed, Jennifer's autonomic nervous system (ANS) does not distinguish between a difficult test and an attacking lion. Either way, the ANS responds by increasing her **(16) heart** rate and respiration, diverting blood from digestion to her skeletal **(17) muscles,** and releasing sugar and fat to prepare her body for **(18) fight** or **(19) flight.**

Driving home after class, Jennifer notices her car is overheating, then sees flames bursting from under the hood. In response to this new stressor, her heart begins to beat wildly and she feels faint, what Hans **(20) Selye** called the alarm reaction or the **(21) general adaptation** syndrome. In the second phase of the syndrome, called **(22) resistance,** she swerves over to the side of the road and leaps out of her car. The firefighters who extinguish the flames also comfort Jennifer, but the combined stresses of the day have led her to the third stage, **(23) exhaustion.** A few days later, Jennifer comes down with a wicked cold, which might be an effect of the stress weakening her **(24) immune** system, including the activity of the **(25) lymphocytes** and **(26) macrophages.**

Review 14.2: Smoking: An Illness-Related Behavior

Malcolm has been trying to quit smoking for years, but it's very difficult. He started smoking during early **(1) adolescence** for two main reasons: He wanted to look cool and grown-up, so he **(2) modeled** his behavior after admired actors he'd seen smoking in movies, and he felt pressured by his **(3) friends** who were already smoking. Today, 20 years later, Malcolm has tried several techniques for quitting (the patch, gum, etc.), but nothing works because he is **(4) dependent** on nicotine. In fact, he now needs two packs instead of one to get the same effect, because he has developed a **(5) tolerance** for the drug. Malcolm's addiction is due to several factors: First, nicotine triggers the release of **(6) epinephrine** and **(7) norepinephrine,** which boosts **(8) alertness** and mental efficiency, abilities that Malcolm feels are important for his work. Second, nicotine stimulates the central nervous system to release **(9) neurotransmitters,** calm **(10) anxiety,** and reduce sensitivity to **(11) pain.** To make matters worse, Malcolm's family and friends, almost all of whom smoke, **(12) will not** support his efforts by quitting with him.

Chapter 15
Personality

Review 15.1: The Psychoanalytic Perspective

Klaus is 18 years old and, like all adolescents, he is trying to figure out who he is. He wants to know why he thinks, feels, and acts the way he does; that is, he wants to define his **(1) personality.** Klaus decides to read about the various personality theorists, beginning with Sigmund **(2) Freud,** who believed that most of the mind is hidden from view and therefore **(3) unconscious,** and that personality is a product of the **(4) conflict** between our basic sexual and aggressive impulses, directed by the **(5) id,** and social restraint derived from the **(6) superego.** After reading about this psychoanalytic theory, Klaus decided that his long-standing aggressive behavior toward his younger brother could have been the result of **(7) repressing** his anger with his parents for being so strict. This would protect him from the **(8) anxiety** he might feel if he were to express that anger. Perhaps the part of his personality called the **(9) ego** redirects his anger, and so the hitting of his brother is a **(10) defense** mechanism called **(11) displacement.** Klaus also thought that he may have **(12) rationalized** his behavior by saying that his brother needed the discipline.

Review 15.2: Neo-Freudians and Psychodynamic Theorists

Klaus isn't sure he agrees with Freud's theory. Klaus thinks that Freud placed too much emphasis on the **(1) unconscious** mind and on sex and **(2) aggression** as all-consuming motives. Instead, Klaus thinks he is more likely to be guided by his **(3) conscious** mind, though he still believes that **(4) social** interactions had a great effect on his behavior. Klaus learns that his beliefs match the neo-Freudian movement. The neo-Freudians emphasized different aspects of personality. Alfred **(5) Adler** emphasized peoples' efforts to overcome feelings of **(6) inferiority.** Karen **(7) Horney** believed that childhood **(8) anxiety** triggers our desire for love and security. Unlike the others, Carl **(9) Jung** agreed with Freud's notion of an **(10) unconscious** but thought it was more of a **(11) collective** unconscious that included images derived from our species' history. Klaus wonders, though, if the modern psychoanalysts—those who profess a **(12) psychodynamic** approach—aren't closer to having a true understanding of personalty. He knows that they **(13) disagree** with Freud's overall personality structure and his classifying people as oral, **(14) anal,** or **(15) phallic,** but they respect the reality that many of our day-to-day thought processes are indeed **(16) unconscious.**

Review 15.3: The Trait Perspective

Denise and Winifred are friends with very different personalities. Unlike Klaus, who wanted the underlying dynamics of his personality **(1) explained,** they simply want their personalities **(2) described,** as trait theorists do. First, Denise and Winifred consider the theory of Hans and Sybil **(3) Eysenck,** who used the statistical procedure of **(4) factor analysis** to reduce our individual variations to two or three dimensions, including **(5) introversion-extraversion** and **(6) stability-instability.** Denise tends to be quiet, reserved, thoughtful, and calm, so she is more likely to be classified as **(7) introverted** and **(8) stable.** Winifred, on the other hand, is outgoing, lively, restless, and impulsive, so she is more likely to be classified as **(9) extraverted** and **(10) unstable.** Winifred and Denise decide to volunteer for neuroscience research on personality in order to learn more. They find evidence that their personalities have a biological basis. For example, they learn that the areas of Winifred's **(11) frontal lobes** involved in behavior inhibition are less active than the same areas in Denise's brain. They also learn that their **(12) genes** played a significant role in creating their **(13) temperament,** which helped define their personalities.

Denise and Winifred decide that these two dimensions are too limiting, so they turn to a more contemporary expanded set of factors, called the **(14) Big Five,** which include Denise's disciplined behavior versus Winifred's impulsive behavior, or **(15) Conscientiousness;** the tendency of both to be soft-hearted and trusting, or **(16) Agreeable;** Denise's calmness versus Winifred's anxiety, or **(17) Neuroticism;** Denise's conformity versus Winifred's imaginative nature, or **(18) Openness;** and Denise's sobriety versus Winifred's sociability, or **(19) Extraversion.** Checking the research, Denise and Winifred find evidence that these trait factors **(20) are** stable in adulthood, they tend to have a 50 percent **(21) heritability** rate, they **(22) do** describe personality in various cultures, and they **(23) do** predict other personality attributes, for example, that Denise is a "lark," or morning type.

Review 15:4: The Social-Cognitive Perspective

Denise and Winifred can't stop thinking about how their personalities are formed. Knowing that psychological science views people as **(1) biopsychosocial** organisms, they set their sights on Albert **(2) Bandura's** theory. This theorist emphasizes the interaction of internal **(3) cognitive** factors, **(4) behavior,** and the environment, a process he called **(5) reciprocal determinism.** The interaction varies between Denise and Winifred for several possible reasons, including the following: They choose different **(6) environments:** Denise might choose to go to the library, while Winifred chooses a coffee shop with friends. Their internal thoughts, or **(7) cognitions,** shape how they interpret and react to events: Denise takes challenges in stride, while Winifred becomes anxious. Their **(8) personalities** create the situations to which they react: Denise shies away from people, while Winifred greets them warmly. According to this theory, how Denise and Winifred react to their environment depends on certain factors, including their sense of **(9) personal control** (hint: internal or external) and their attributional style (**(10) optimistic** or **(11) pessimistic**). Finally, both Denise and Winifred learn the importance of maintaining a positive attitude and building on their strengths, based on the research of Martin **(12) Seligman,** which indicates that optimal human functioning benefits health.

Chapter 16
Psychological Disorders

Review 16.1: Anxiety Disorders

Carol almost constantly feels extremely tense and uneasy for no apparent reason. She cannot concentrate on her studies, and she's on the verge of failing all her courses. This suggests that she may suffer from a **(1) generalized anxiety** disorder, which may lead to **(2) physical** problems, such as ulcers and high blood pressure. Because Carol cannot identify the cause of her tension, it would be described by Sigmund **(3) Freud** as **(4) free-floating,** while learning theorists would link her anxiety with **(5) classical conditioning** of fear, and biological psychologists might link it to an overarousal of **(6) brain** areas involved in **(7) impulse** control. Carol's roommate Shayna complains of similar feelings, but also experiences unexpected episodes of intense dread, known as **(8) panic** attacks, which are accompanied by physical symptoms such as heart **(9) palpitations,** shortness of breath, and choking sensations. Shayna has experienced several of these frightening episodes and has begun to avoid situations in which she fears **(10) escape** may be difficult. Thus, Shayna is developing a fear of leaving her home, which may become **(11) agoraphobia** if the feelings intensify. Carol and Shayna's friend Randal doesn't understand their inability to identify the source of their anxiety. He says, "I know exactly what I fear: heights. I have a **(12) phobia,** which I know is **(13) irrational,** but at least I can deal with it by avoiding tall buildings, for example. I believe I **(14) learned** my fear from my dad, after watching him fall off our roof and never climbing a ladder again."

While Randal is talking with Carol and Shayna, another friend Moira is making her third trip to the restroom to wash her hands. Moira has become **(15) obsessed** with the idea that doorknobs or any objects handled by others are full of germs. By giving in to her **(16) compulsion** to wash her hands, she eliminates the germs. But this constant hand-washing is interfering with her everyday life. One useful explanation for Moira's behavior is biological: Brain scans have shown that an area that monitors our actions and checks for errors, the **(17) anterior cingulate** cortex, is especially likely to be hyperactive in people with Moira's disorder. Alternatively, learning theorists would say that actions such as frequent hand-washing reduce a sufferer's **(18) anxiety,** thus reinforcing the hand-washing. As they talk, the four friends remember Shayna's brother Shawn, who is an Army lieutenant serving in Afghanistan. In his many e-mails, he has described to Shayna some horrific situations. Shayna fears that when Shawn returns, he will have nightmares and suffer other constant reminders of the horrors he has seen, which would be symptoms of **(19) post-traumatic stress** disorder. As explained by **(20) learning** theorists, any reminders of his war-time experiences will bring out feelings of **(21) anxiety.**

Review 16.2: Mood Disorders

Dwayne's parents (Isabel and Max) are worried about him. Dwayne's fiancée Arlene recently died in a car accident and since then Dwayne has been lethargic and has lost all interest in family and friends. This behavior has lasted for more than two weeks, suggesting that he is suffering from **(1) major depressive** disorder, which is more common in **(2) women** than in **(3) men.** Isabel and Max think there may be a biological explanation for Dwayne's condition. They recall that Isabel's mother and sister were both diagnosed with psychological problems, indicating a **(4) genetic** influence. However, a psychologist with a **(5) social-cognitive** perspective suggests that Dwayne's **(6) self-defeating** beliefs and **(7) negative** explanatory style may also be contributing to his inability to get over the loss of his fiancée. After about a month, Dwayne comes out of his room, all excited with plans to move to Hawaii and start a new career in real estate. Max and Isabel's psychologist suggests that these symptoms may indicate the presence of **(8) bipolar** disorder, which is characterized by alternating mood swings between **(9) depression** and the overexcited state of **(10) mania.** Researchers have found that during bipolar episodes of depression, brain levels of **(11) norepinephrine** and **(12) serotonin** are low, and one of these neurotransmitters, **(13) norepinephrine,** is overabundant during bipolar episodes of mania.

Review 16.3: Schizophrenia

The Swiss Guards are blocking his way, but Trevor insists that he be let in: "I am the Pope," he says. Trevor is experiencing a **(1) delusion,** which is a common symptom of **(2) schizophrenia.** Other symptoms include the following: The voices Trevor hears that tell him he is Pope and that he must "say the Mass this morning" are auditory **(3) hallucinations.** Trevor also laughs hysterically when the Guard points a gun at him, thus exhibiting **(4) inappropriate** emotions. Given the presence of odd behaviors, Trevor's symptoms are considered **(5) positive,** and they seem to indicate that he has **(6) paranoid** schizophrenia. Trevor has been in and out of psychiatric hospitals since he was a teenager, indicating that he suffers from **(7) chronic,** or process, schizophrenia and that his chances of recovery are **(8) poor.** Researchers have proposed several explanations for schizophrenia. One explanation involves low brain activity in the **(9) frontal lobe** and a noticeable decline in the brain waves that reflect **(10) synchronized** neural firing. An alternative explanation suggests that a mid-pregnancy **(11) viral** infection impairs brain development in the fetus. Schizophrenia is largely influenced by genetic and biochemical factors, but extreme stress often triggers the disorder, which indicates that **(12) environment** also plays a role in its onset.

Chapter 17
Therapy

Review 17.1 : Psychoanalysis

At his friends' urging, Barney has decided to seek help for the depression he has been been struggling with ever since moving away from home and starting college two months ago. He's heard a lot about Sigmund **(1) Freud's** therapy, called **(2) psychoanalysis,** in which patients use **(3) free association** to express whatever comes to mind in order to uncover their **(4) repressed** unconscious conflicts. In this therapy, analysts traditionally would interpret their patients' tendency to change the subject in response to difficult questions as **(5) resistance,** and if a patient's anger toward abusive family members began to be directed at the therapist, that defense would be interpreted as **(6) transference.** Barney finds, however, that this therapy is practiced by only a very few therapists and that most are instead offering an updated version called **(7) psychodynamic** therapy. In this therapy, current symptoms are analyzed to consider themes across important **(8) relationships,** such as those between Barney and his family members back home. Or, Barney might be helped best by the brief variation known as **(9) interpersonal** psychotherapy, which may enable him to gain **(10) insight** into the root of his problem.

Review 17.2: Humanistic Therapies

Megan has been researching the history of therapy and has become fascinated by the therapies that emphasize people's inherent potential for **(1) self-fulfillment,** which are known as **(2) humanistic** therapies. These therapies have several important characteristics that differentiate them from psychoanalysis, including focusing on the **(3) present and future** rather than on the **(4) past,** promoting **(5) growth** in their clients rather than trying to cure **(6) illnesses,** and emphasizing **(7) conscious** rather than **(8) unconscious** thoughts. Megan further learns that therapists such as Carl **(9) Rogers,** who founded **(10) client-centered** therapy, encouraged all therapists to exhibit **(11) genuineness**—expressing their true feelings, **(12) acceptance**—allowing clients to feel unconditional positive regard, and **(13) empathy**—sensing and reflecting their clients' feelings. Together, these features form Rogers' concept of **(14) active listening.**

Review 17.3: Behavior Therapies

Trish recently moved across Canada for her studies, but she is so afraid of flying that she now rarely sees her family and friends at home. This fear is interfering with her life, so Trish decides to seek help from a therapist who uses **(1) classical** conditioning principles to pair the stimulus that triggers her fear (flying) with a new response that is incompatible with that fear (relaxation), which is referred to as **(2) counterconditioning.** The therapist proposes a technique called systematic **(3) desensitization,** which is a type of **(4) exposure** therapy that pairs **(5) relaxation** with gradually increasing **(6) anxiety**-triggering stimuli (going to the airport, going to the gate, getting on the plane, learning about flight procedures, actually taking a flight). However, Trish is embarrassed by the idea of exposing her fears in public (at the airport). So, the therapist suggests **(7) virtual reality** exposure therapy, which would allow Trish to work through her fears by way of vivid, three-dimensional, computer **(8) simulations.**

Review 17.4: Cognitive Therapy for Depression

Lola is searching for a therapist. After her father and mother divorced, and he moved away, she began reading about cognitive therapies, hoping those techniques might help her move on with her life. Lola learned that one famous cognitive therapist, Aaron **(1) Beck,** analyzed the dreams of depressed people and found recurring themes of loss and rejection. This famous psychologist's goal in therapy was to reverse clients' **(2) catastrophizing** beliefs by questioning their **(3) irrational** thinking. Lola decides to try an approach in which she will be trained to alter the way she acts (**(4) behavior** therapy) and the way she thinks (**(5) cognitive** therapy). This **(6) integrated** approach is called **(7) cognitive-behavior** therapy. Lola's friend Moira has been undergoing treatment using this therapeutic approach for her obsession with germs and her compulsive hand-washing. Moira is learning to **(8) relabel** her compulsive thoughts about germs. For example, she says to herself, "I am having a compulsive urge that is due to my **(9) brain's** abnormal activity. Instead of giving in to the urge to wash my hands, I will engage in an alternative **(10) behavior,** such as taking a walk."

Review 17.5: Biomedical Therapies

Jessica's therapist has diagnosed her with major depressive disorder and has suggested that her recovery may be expedited if she takes an **(1) antidepressant** drug such as Prozac. Because her therapist is a **(2) psychiatrist,** he can prescribe drugs to his patients. Unlike the **(3) antianxiety** drugs, which depress central nervous system activity, these drugs work by increasing the availability of **(4) norepinephrine** or **(5) serotonin,** which are neurotransmitters that elevate **(6) mood** and arousal and are **(7) scarce** in depression. Prozac is called a **(8) selective-serotonin-reuptake** inhibitor (SSRI) because it partially blocks the reabsorption of **(9) serotonin** from neural **(10) synapses.** If the drugs and psychotherapy together don't work for Jessica, her therapist may suggest the most controversial treatment for depression, **(11) electroconvulsive therapy,** which involves sending a brief electrical current through the patient's brain. Alternatively, Jessica might try **(12) repetitive transcranial magnetic** stimulation (rTMS), which produces fewer side effects such as **(13) seizures** or **(14) memory** loss.

Chapter 18
Social Psychology

Review 18.1: Social Thinking

Aimee sees Monica—a girl from her class whom she doesn't know except by name—running out of a jewelry store. Aimee thinks, "She must have stolen something and is running away." Aimee shares that suspicion with some friends. Aimee is **(1) attributing** Monica's behavior to her **(2) disposition.** In fact, Monica got a phone call saying that her Mom had been rushed to the hospital, and she was racing to meet her there. Her behavior was actually due to the **(3) situation,** and so Aimee had made the **(4) fundamental attribution** error. The idea that people usually attribute others' behavior either to their **(5) internal** dispositions or to their **(6) external** situations was proposed by Fritz **(7) Heider.** Because Aimee's incorrect beliefs about Monica are negative, she is predisposed to develop a negative **(8) attitude** toward Monica and to behave accordingly if other influences are **(9) minimal,** her attitude is **(10) specific** to the behavior, and she is keenly **(11) aware** of her feelings. When Aimee learns the truth about Monica's behavior, she experiences **(12) cognitive dissonance,** because her new understanding now conflicts with her past behaviors.

Review 18.2: Social Influence

Calvin does not belong to a fraternity. His friend Theo has pledged with Omega Psi. Although they once were close, they have drifted apart because Theo is **(1) conforming** his thinking and behavior to the standards set by his fraternity brothers. Research by Solomon **(2) Asch** identified factors that may have contributed to Theo's changed behavior, including the following: Theo was made to feel **(3) incompetent** by upperclassmen when he was pledging. The other Omega Psi fraternity brothers were **(4) unanimous** in their views. Theo **(5) admired** Omega Psi's status and attractiveness on campus. Changing his behavior in order to gain his fraternity brothers' approval meant that Theo was succumbing to **(6) normative** social influence. David, the president of Theo's fraternity, has ordered all pledges to befriend only fellow fraternity brothers. Because David is considered a legitimate **(7) authority** figure, Theo obeys his order. As Stanley **(8) Milgram's** research results would predict, Theo refuses to associate with Calvin, who does not belong to his fraternity. Theo's fraternity sets the social **(9) standard (norm)** for brothers' behavior, and not one brother veers from the rules, so there are no **(10) role models** for defiance.

Review 18.3: Social Relations

Two new biology majors, Wynona and Jason, have been hired as work-study students in the lab. The amount of time they spend in close **(1) proximity** is a powerful predictor that they will at least develop a friendship. As the days and months go by, their liking for each other will most likely increase. This is because of the **(2) mere exposure** effect, which according to **(3) evolutionary** psychologists is adaptive; our ancestors survived because they found that what was different was potentially dangerous, and what was **(4) familiar** was safe. Wynona and Jason also find each other **(5) attractive,** which contributes to their budding relationship. Wynona and Jason begin dating and, as they get to know each other, their liking increases because they **(6) share** interests and values. Also, because they both feel that the benefits of their relationship outweigh the costs, the **(7) reward** theory predicts that the relationship will grow and develop. Using the **(8) two-factor** theory of emotion to explain what has now become passionate love between Jason and Wynona, Elaine **(9) Hatfield** would identify the ingredients of their love as physical **(10) arousal** and cognitive **(11) appraisal.** With time, their passionate love may develop into **(12) companionate** love, which is characterized by equal giving and receiving by both partners, or **(13) equity,** and by both revealing their dreams and worries, or **(14) self-disclosure.**